A Horse at Night

Art on cover:
Augustus Leopold Egg, *The Travelling Companions*, 1862

ISBN: 978-1-948980-13-5

The publisher wishes to thank Edil Hassan and Sebastian Mazza.

Library of Congress Cataloging-in-Publication Data
Names: Cain, Amina, author.
Title: A horse at night: on writing / Amina Cain.
Description: St. Louis, MO: Dorothy, a publishing project, [2022] |
Identifiers: LCCN 2022013859 (print) | LCCN 2022013860 (ebook) | ISBN
    9781948980135 (paperback) | ISBN 9781948980142 (ebook)
Subjects: LCSH: Cain, Amina. | Novelists, American—21st
    century—Biography. | Cain, Amina—Books and reading. |
    Fiction—Authorship—Psychological aspects. | Art appreciation. | LCGFT:
    Autobiographies. | Essays.
Classification: LCC PS3603.A3788 Z46 2022 (print) | LCC PS3603.A3788
    (ebook) | DDC 818/603 [B]—dc23/eng/20220427
LC record available at https://lccn.loc.gov/2022013859
LC ebook record available at https://lccn.loc.gov/2022013860

Design and composition by Danielle Dutton
Printed on permanent, durable, acid-free recycled paper in the United States of America

Dorothy, a publishing project books are distributed to the trade by New York Review Books

Dorothy, a publishing project | St. Louis, MO
DOROTHYPROJECT.COM

A Horse at Night
— *On Writing* —

Amina Cain

Dorothy, a publishing project

To my mother, Deborah Lou Miner, artist and adventurer

CONTENTS

WITHOUT PLANNING IT, I WROTE a diary of sorts. Lightly. A diary of fiction. Or is that not what this is? I wrote about reading fiction, and about writing it. Sometimes I read and thought about the books my friends had written (they were my friends partly because I felt great kinship with what they wrote), sometimes about books by writers I will never know. They are dead, or they are alive, but still I won't meet them. It is enough to read their work.

Yet, I have never kept a diary. Or I have tried, but it never stuck. Again and again I would begin: with a very short entry, or else with a long one that would come to stand on its own, there in the beginning of a notebook, followed by all of those blank pages. I don't know if, when I wrote essays, I was actually returning to the same space, if somehow I had managed to get back to those empty pages, managed to get back to a pasture of thought. And now that it is done, I am keeping a real diary for the first time in my life, or is it a pasture, mostly because when I can't, or don't have time, to work on my novel, I can still write there. Sometimes I trick myself when writing in my notebook; sometimes I end up working on the novel after all, in those pages. And that is the best reason to return to it, that it brings me closer to something I haven't otherwise been able to get to, or that can't get to me. I want to go further into my writing, into my thinking. *"And do I?"*

*

I DROVE TO THE LITTLE SHOP when it was getting dark. I bought pears, persimmons, chard, butter, and ice cream. At home, I had already made potato leek soup. We know what Marguerite Duras said about leek soup.

Imagine surrounding your own soup. Imagine surrounding it with anguish.

At night I am surrounded by my books, not the one I am writing.

I wanted to write fiction because I saw something in Duras's Lol Stein. I didn't know how to stop thinking about that
character. Lol doesn't know how to stop thinking about her
rejection by Michael Richardson, and I had a lot of ideas
about rejection, as I'd been rejected by a few people myself.
I had rejected others, but I didn't think about that as much.
It didn't hold the same fascination. I wanted to read about
long walks in the summer when no one else is out on the
street, the ocean not in view, necessarily, but near. I read *The
Ravishing of Lol Stein* for the first time when I was in my
late twenties. Then again in my late forties. I read *The Lost
Daughter* by Elena Ferrante the second time in my late forties too; the first time had been a few years before that. In
the same summer, I re-read them both. They made me long
for summer right as I was experiencing it, a double immersion—fiction and life—that I enjoyed. In *The Lost Daughter*,
it is Leda who does the rejecting so she can spend her summer alone, working and swimming.

I had taken my own long walks on hot emptied streets.
I had walked near a lake that wasn't quite in view, like Lol's
wide river in South Tahla, and the memory of Town Beach.
Now when I walk, it is the ocean that is somewhere in the

distance. I have to drive thirty minutes to see it. Now I am walking with the mountains near me. The desert is in the opposite direction from the ocean.

Mountains or water or desert, the heat burns things away. A special kind of cleanse.

One reads or writes a novel like one goes out to walk in the heat, or into the rain, to buy the persimmon and the butter.

The little shop, I have gone to it a couple of times a week every week for many years. Can you picture me driving there, all that I was thinking, all that I was feeling? Picture it one hundred times. On this day this person was important to me, on this day another. Often it was the same person, the same people. There was something I needed from the shop, or I wanted to leave my desk. I don't think it's bad to leave your desk, especially when you are going to a place that reminds you of the shop Laura discovers in Sylvia Townsend Warner's *Lolly Willowes*, the one that is half florist, half green grocer. And so I have also always been thinking of Lolly.

The flowers that look like bright yellow balls, with soft little pinetree-like leaves, are standing in their bucket of water, not far from a large bowl of tangerines. Fresh flowers, and surrounded by darkness in that corner. How could I not think of Lolly, especially in the blustery seasons? I was glad I left my commonplace desk. I went back to it with those images in my mind.

For me, fiction is a space of plainness and of excess.

"Lol stirred, she turned over in her sleep. Lol went out for walks through the streets, she learned to walk without having any special goal in mind." Reading it, I am happy. You might think that is simple. Now I know that I have always been here to see Lol, and that I always will be. One day my portrait will be painted, seeing her. That is what my gaze will symbolize. The gaze does symbolize. And not just seeing Lol, but Leda, in the water, walking through that beach town or at a fish market, and Lolly, finding her pleasure and her freedom in the Chilterns. Pleasure, freedom, torment, emptiness: it is what I want my writing to express. I don't know if I have ever actually expressed it.

You were in a rage, and then you were calm. You hid things, but you were real.

These characters whose names begin with L.

*

FOR YEARS NOW, WHENEVER I READ a short story or a novel, narrative has been impressing itself more and more visually in my mind. Or maybe it's that my mind has gone more and more toward these fictional visions. Even though I'm a writer, it's not always language I'm drawn to first. When I start writing a new story, I often begin with setting. Before plot, before dialogue, before anything else, I begin to see where a story will take place, and then I hear the narrative voice, which means that character is not far behind. Lately I've been thinking a lot about landscape painting and literature, and perhaps as an extension of this I have started to think through the idea of character and landscape as similar things, or at least as intimates, co-dependent.

In *I Await the Devil's Coming*, Mary MacLane writes, "We three go out on the sand and barrenness: my wooden heart, my good young woman's-body, my soul . . . this sand and barrenness forms the setting for the personality of me." This is a gentle Mary MacLane, not the caustic one, going sadly out into her Montana landscape (she would rather be in the city). Taking the reader there too. Taking the reader to her personality. For where are we when we read Mary MacLane? We are in the three things that form her *and* we are in the sand. I would like to visit MacLane's Montana in the same way I would like to visit the wasted, spectral landscape in Paul Delvaux's 1937 painting *The Lamps* (those gray, crumbling hills), partly so I might meet the five identical figures who haunt it, trudging across that land.

It's *Anna Karenina* that Orhan Pamuk returns to again and again in his book *The Naïve and the Sentimental Novelist*, as a character formed by her surroundings. Anna makes an impression on the reader not simply because of how Tolstoy has drawn her, Pamuk argues, but because she has been drawn as part of a brilliant landscape, not detached from it. To look out of the train window while Anna looks out of it too. To see Anna as the train and the snowy landscape, or at least made of the same cloth. I think this is what excites me about narrative. Outside the body and inside the mind, a novel can be like a landscape painting with a character moving through it, all of her violences and joys playing themselves out in only this setting, only this narrative, for in another it would not be so.

In Renee Gladman's *Ana Patova Crosses a Bridge*, the third novel in her series on the invented city-state of Ravicka, it's not just buildings that form the landscape of the book, but the sentence itself, which is alive and fashions its own kind of architecture. "The story wasn't given to me as most are, as some kind of choreography beaten against the body rather it was laid on top of my voice." I am reading *Ana Patova Crosses a Bridge*, not watching it, but I see this so clearly: invisible words laid on top of a voice. A kind of drawing too—drawn lightly, perhaps. We get to this image, this way of being alive, this sort of architecture, through narrative. Like we get to the territory of Mary MacLane.

Recently, while working on a short story, I kept seeing its setting in the same way its narrator sees setting in the paintings she looks at when she visits a museum. It was natural then to write them in the same way, and also that they would, in some sense, join. The narrator of this story is always gazing *at* landscape (in paintings) and she is always *in* landscape (her own). She takes pleasure in each, and sometimes they give her trouble, but still she seems to live in both. When she looks at the paintings, they allow her to emerge into another kind of place, even though the physical space around her hasn't actually changed.

There is the woman in green in Marie NDiaye's *Self-Portrait in Green*, and a line of all the other women in green who come after: a woman who may or may not be the narrator's friend, Cristina; the narrator's mother; her father's fifth or sixth wife; Jenny, and Jenny's ex-husband's new wife. It is an unusual book, hard to describe, even harder to categorize, but the figure of the "woman in green" is at the center of it, a kind of woman that might be any woman, who doubles and then doubles again, and is perhaps Marie NDiaye herself. That first woman in green is always near, or merged with, a banana tree. The narrator sees her while driving past the same farmhouse day after day. Or is she not seeing her? She isn't sure if the woman is real. One day she asks her children if they see her too, and they say they do not. "Are you sure?" she asks them, and shivers. The tree is lovely; it is the only tree in the yard. Still, it can't be separated from the woman who haunts it. "I said to myself, 'that woman in green has always been there.'" When I think of that book, I always see that image of a banana tree with a woman who may or may not be standing next to it.

What does a reader do with these literary landscapes? Is it enough just to see them? Pamuk suggests that to link them creates more than an aesthetic experience, that there is something to be gained in that linking, that in doing so we ourselves are moving outside of our own borders, able to more deeply apprehend our connection to all that exists. "In this way, the novelist comes to resemble those ancient Chinese painters who climbed mountain peaks in order to capture the poetry of vast landscapes." But what if you are a short story writer or a novelist interested in something other than story? What if when you look at a piece of art there is something in it you want to try in writing, because to you it seems as if a story should be able to hold something like that, hold possibilities, not exclude them.

Claire Donato's novel *Burial* makes visible a world of disorientation the death of a father must bring. It's a *mind* made into a *place*, not unlike a setting, but it's more than that. Remarkably, this life of the mind is sometimes sensual. How is it that a death place could in any way be inviting? "It is not snowing so heavily now, though what is not seen is always meant to break. Human beings are made of ice, crystals that fall through the body, freeze until they melt, discharge, and then detach atop the ice atop the lake." Is the body a lake? Here, the two are made of the same thing; one of them falls through to the other. It is easy to see this passage of the narrative as a landscape painting, one that has the potential to be comforting, even if you think it shouldn't. The fact that it can do this invites us in.

I remember the first time I encountered the work of the artist Bill Viola at a retrospective at the Art Institute of Chicago. I walked through the dark galleries, videos installed everywhere, and it was like I was in a haunted house, large screens with their larger-than-life projections. Afterward, I went home and immediately wanted to write. It's not that I wanted to write a story about Viola's work, or even based on it. I wanted to write *to* something in the work, or I wanted to reproduce in writing some quality I had seen there. Some years after, I saw a video clip by Viola on YouTube, *I Do Not Know What It Is I Am Like* (1986), the one of the owl toward which the camera gets closer and closer, until the camera person (Viola?) is reflected in the owl's eyes. The video is very short, barely three minutes, and it is not a story, or even story-like, yet there is something in it I'd like to do too, in a story.

What is it that happens when a narrative allows us to look at an image longer than we are "supposed" to, when it is just as interesting as the story being told? Can a performance of character rest there? I think about Anna Karenina and the train, superimposed on top of each other, all the humanity present in that image, racing through the snow; the three things that make Mary MacLane in her empty Montana sandscape; a crystal lake and a frozen body; a woman in green and a banana tree; one thing laid on top of another. Together, not separate. Relaxing into each other with their outlines intact.

*

I RECENTLY READ, AND LOVED, Annie Ernaux's *The Possession*. But what did I love, exactly? Its urgency, I suppose. The way the narrator is taken over by something, her obsessive jealousy over her ex-lover's new live-in girlfriend. Ernaux does obsession and jealousy very well: crude, angry, a little violent. Sometimes it feels as though the novella's sentences are a series of hits or punches. Here is one: "The first thing I did after waking up was grab his cock—stiff with sleep—and hold still, as if hanging onto a branch." I'm struck by the gesture, as I am by the idea that writers can gesture in this way through the sentence, leaving a mark on the reader. Here is another: "I decided that I hated all female professors—though I myself had been one, and many of my friends still were."

Of all the forms language can take, the sentence is the one I'm most drawn to. Since my phrasing is plain and spare (as writer Caren Beilin once asked me, can a sentence be a Shaker room?), I didn't always think it was. Long, rich, complicated sentences in which a surprise is hidden—I thought whoever wrote them were the real sentence writers. And they are; I love to read such sentences. But I see now that I hide things in my sentences too. I thought because I write slim books, I was already working within the smallest unit possible, which is a unit I like, where I write best. Now I see that sometimes my focus gets even smaller, and that I am not always writing a sentence to tell a story, exactly, but simply to be in the space of a sentence, to make things appear in it, to see what is possible.

I find it enjoyable to make objects appear, and characters appear, which is different than how the characters *look*. And when objects and characters, and also landscapes, appear together, that is another way narrative happens for me. It seems possible that it's partly how Lisa Robertson's *The Baudelaire Fractal* came together. Or Susan Finlay's *Objektophilia*, both of which are rich in objects, rich in their sentences. I would rather work in front of or behind a narrative, where I can focus on these other things even if the story is still there. I want to leave a chain of images that remain in the reader's mind. I want to write what heightened experience feels like.

In the short story "Olimpia's Ghost," from Sofia Samatar's collection *Tender*, the narrator Gisela has wild theatrical dreams after reading E.T.A. Hoffmann's "The Sandman" before bed, then describes those dreams in letters to a young Sigmund Freud. Her dreams bring into existence a new reality, fictional and psychological, born from the images and objects of Hoffmann's tales; in other words, the images and objects of literature. She is marked by them. Declaring her too sensitive for Hoffmann, Sigmund enlists Gisela's brother Emil to take the book away from her, which he does, sheepishly. "When he left me, and I moved at last, raising my hand to smooth my hair, my own shadow startled me, shifting on the wall." A simple image, and a simple moment, but it creates the *sense* of another actuality, a glimpse of a shadow world.

In my own fiction, I sometimes find myself trying to conjure something that isn't there, so that it both is and isn't appearing. For instance, in my novel *Indelicacy*, when the narrator Vitória is visiting the desert, she says, "I pulled my hair into a loose bun, but not like a dancer would do it." There is no dancer in this sentence, yet I see the dancer. This is one way to haunt a sentence. Plainly. It is exciting to me to think I might haunt my own sentences, to believe that they can be haunted. That the reader might be taken over subtly, that there is room in fiction for an experience like this. And that something of this experience might remain.

*

In *the lost daughter*, when leda goes alone to the sea on her summer vacation, she thinks of her daughters, far away in Toronto with their father, and doesn't miss them. Instead she becomes focused on the drama of another family she sees every day at the beach, especially on Nina, a young woman at the center of that family. Without them knowing, Leda intrudes on the family; she intensifies their drama. For a time she becomes a confidante to the young woman, giving her advice that is dark but also direct, intimate. At one point Leda says to Nina: "Sometimes you have to escape in order not to die."

The ocean is many things, of course, one of them a screen, something we watch from the beach while absentmindedly projecting our thoughts upon it. Or we read a book and when we look out at the horizon the book appears there too. When we swim, most of us stay fairly close to the shore. Farther out and the projection grows thinner. We project onto something, not *in*. When Leda is in front of the sea it is her own life, her flawed, complicated self, rather than her absent family, that is placed on top of it.

But why do we project at all? One hot day last summer I went with some friends to El Matador Beach in Malibu, and the particular blueness of the water that afternoon made me feel I was somewhere tropical, or maybe I just wanted to be. While I enjoyed myself, talking and eating with my friends, and swimming, there was a part of me that was imagining we were at some other beach in some other place. I was projecting one ocean on top of another. I should have stayed present: El Matador is stunning after all, with rocky cliffs that rise up sharply from the narrow beach. Succulents and cacti and wildflowers and chaparral and sage grow there. You can see them as you make your way down the steep steps to the water.

It was the ocean of my early childhood in Florida I was projecting, where the water was clear and warm, with lush plants growing beyond the beach, saw palmetto and mangrove trees. And beyond them, marshes and swamps. And I was seeing beaches I haven't yet visited but want to, in Costa Rica and Martinique. The beaches I am dreaming of.

For better or worse, I have always combined one place with another, lived in one landscape while dreaming of a second. It used to be the desert I constantly imagined and wrote about when I lived in Chicago; sometimes it still is. The desert isn't blank and neither is the ocean, but in their vastness they are relaxing as if they were. Plants are relaxing as well, but for different reasons. And so plants that grow in or near the desert or ocean are doubly so.

There are the empty settings of certain Duras novels, *The Ravishing of Lol Stein* among them. When Lol walks around her neighborhood, she projects onto it over and over that moment from her past, the ball at Town Beach when Michael Richardson leaves her for Anne-Marie Stretter. After he is gone, she herself is so empty you would think she isn't affected at all, but that betrayal and that emptiness exist together easily in the rest of the book. Sometimes the betrayal appears without drama on top of the emptiness; sometimes the betrayal is the surface.

> What Lol would have liked would have been to have the ball immured, to make of it this ship of light upon which, each afternoon, she embarks, but which remains there, in this impossible port, forever anchored and yet ready to sail away with its three passengers from this entire future in which Lol Stein now takes her place.

We project onto people; we attach one person to another. We haven't been able to let go of the first person, and try to connect them to a second. We're either aware we're doing this, or we're not. We project our own self, what we want and what we want another person to be. We project what we fear, or what we dislike. Sometimes it's reversed: we take on someone's intonation, without even trying. We dress like them, or copy something we saw them do. We try to bring a projection of them onto our own selves.

Since reading the novel *Hot Milk* by Deborah Levy, I've been imagining that sea in Southern Spain where the narrator Sofia is stung twice by several jellyfish. The medusas in the water in Almería are transparent and have long tentacles. The land beyond that sea: a scorched desert with white plastic greenhouses scattered across the hills. I like to imagine the medusas and the greenhouses are communicating with each other, projecting themselves to each other across the beach.

In Joanna Walsh's "Vagues" from her book *Vertigo*, a narrator sits in an oyster restaurant with a man who is not her husband, though it seems her husband is projected into the scene in the way she thinks of him. We see also the objects in the restaurant and the other people, the beach and the water, for the story is especially cinematic. The narrator (facing away from the ocean) sits across from the man who is not her husband and thinks: "Now he is here, seated at the table that looks out at the sea. It is the table he indicated, the table he desired, from which he can see the sea the beach the seagulls the stork the mother the stones the toddler the seaweed the rubbish, and at the other side of the table interrupting his view of all these things, me."

Whether in art or writing, I'm drawn continuously to these projections, when one thing is placed on top of another without eclipsing it. Like two different time periods: both are present, and together they form something new. Or two different cities. In that way it's neither, but someplace else. We project sentences onto the blank pages of our notebooks, onto the screens of our laptops. What we see in our minds we make real.

Predictably, the tropics appear in the novel I am writing now, the plants of the tropics, and the ocean. I project what I want, what I'm obsessed with, onto my writing more than any other place. It's an act I'm aware of. When I project onto people, I imagine I mostly don't know I'm doing it. We have such blind spots. It's strange and probably annoying to the people to whom we're closest that our projections can be virtually invisible to us even when everyone else can see them clearly. We are making images for others that we ourselves can't see. If only we could capture them somehow, make them into films, so that we could watch them too.

In her short experimental movies, the artist/filmmaker Laida Lertxundi very often places one image on top of another, boldly or more subtly, creating a dark unfolding, or a bright one. How striking the images are when they combine, how satisfying. We see how it can be good for things to exist together, and to be able to experience them like that. Once again I arrive at what I love most about art, about writing. How things appear, and the richness of appearances. We ourselves come into view, everywhere we go, with other people, with objects, in landscapes. Hannah Arendt writes in *The Life of the Mind* that, "Living things *make their appearance* like actors on a stage." It's the only way I'm comfortable with thinking of people as objects; it's why I like fashion.

You could say that projecting means we aren't present with what's actually before us, and that would probably be true. But it might also be true that we are sometimes present to something else. When I lived at Tassajara Zen Mountain Center in Carmel Valley, CA for a summer, we were discouraged from listening to music, which was seen as a possible escape. Almost every evening after dinner I listened to it anyway, on headphones, while walking in the mountains in the Ventana wilderness on my own, and every evening I felt elated. I knew I would enjoy the moment even without the music, but together the mountains and the walking and the dusk and the music became something else, and I wasn't willing to give it up. Maybe at some other point in my life I'll want to, or I'll better understand what it means to be present in a way that's pure.

Reading, all on its own, is one of the best things, and yet isn't it nice to read in bed at the end of a long day, the darkness of the window meeting the soft light inside the room? Or on the beach, the hot sand and the sound of the waves coming together with the book. Things combine to become other things, other kinds of experiences.

A final scene, now on the Costa Brava in Roberto Bolaño's *The Third Reich,* begins like this: "Through the window comes the murmur of the sea mingled with the laughter of the night's last revelers, a sound that might be the waiters clearing the tables on the terrace, an occasional car driving slowly along the Paseo Marítimo, and a low and unidentifiable hum from the other rooms in the hotel." As *The Third Reich* goes on there will be a disappearance, mind/war games, and a kind of madness, though this opening sentence is empty and clear. The sea mixed with these other things, but constant. Soon it will be thoroughly visible and the novel will be projected upon it.

*

SOMETIMES A TITLE COMES EASILY, but often it doesn't. I'll think I've found a good one, and get excited about it, but when I run it by my friends I receive an immediate no. My list of rejected titles is long. I feel they should come to me naturally, yet a sentence is so much easier. Even a paragraph is easier. An entire scene.

Many of my favorite books have incomparable titles, and some of them have titles that are not actually very good. Yet somehow they survived. I'm not sure I should name the titles I don't like, but here are my favorites. When I first learn of a title I love, I am immediately jealous. I wish it were mine.

Known and Strange Things by Teju Cole
A Breath of Life by Clarice Lispector
2666 by Roberto Bolaño
The Middle Notebookes by Nathanaël
Hangsaman by Shirley Jackson
Picnic at Hanging Rock by Joan Lindsay
Hurricane Season by Fernanda Melchor
Aug 9—Fog by Kathryn Scanlan
Aiding and Abetting by Muriel Spark
Ban en Banlieue by Bhanu Kapil

Why do I like them? Each one for a different reason, of course, and there is no formula, but still: they are clear-eyed, or enigmatic. They have presence, or they make something new. In a way, they are artworks in miniature, like miniature paintings: each conjures something strong, a microcosm I couldn't have foreseen, but which I immediately want to go into. For a title *can* make you want to go into a book, to read it. A good title offers something acute without being obvious, without giving something away.

*

WHEN I WAS A TEENAGER IN OHIO, I dreamed regularly of leaving, and my daydreams were almost entirely made up of me walking around a city by myself, never with another person, or I was in an apartment alone at night making myself a meal. For a time I wanted to live in Manhattan, and in my mind I saw it like the camera sees it in Chantal Akerman's *News From Home*, that film made up of beautifully held long shots of New York City. In certain scenes, you hear only the sounds of the city, and then the voiceover comes in, like a wave that flows warmly over everything, insistent, and mesmerizing in that insistence, and then is gone. The text of this voiceover is made up of letters Akerman's mother sent her from Belgium, and the voice is Akerman's, so that you are hearing her voice, and these letters that are addressed to her, but you never see her. Rather you see through her eyes. The letters seem as if they are for you, and in this way you are alone in that city too. For me, *News From Home* embodies solitude.

I don't know why I imagined those scenes of myself alone so often. Though it's true I like solitude, I also like spending time with people, and I've only lived alone twice, both times for less than a year. I suppose it was because I was imagining my *own* relationship to something, to escape, to self-determination. It would be me who left my small Ohio city, the only person ever to have made this exact journey. I wanted desperately to choose what my life would look like, not what had been chosen for me. I saw the world then as a warm and open place, full of possibility, and I wanted to experience as much of it as I could.

When another person is accompanying you, they fill the space between you and certain kinds of experience. It is important that that not always happen. A person should be like Ralph Waldo Emerson's transparent eyeball, absorbing everything around them. We can't see in quite this way with someone else by our side.

The first time I left the US, to go to China for three months, I felt like that eyeball, walking around Beijing at dusk, jet-lagged, the neon signs flashing in the street. How exhilarating to finally be in another country. It had taken me quite a while to do it. Later, walking along the Bund in Shanghai, looking at the water and the buildings that ran alongside it, I felt close to some energy I hadn't encountered before: a combination of the newness, for me, of China, and my own self, in it. I became new in China too. I'm sure I would have felt good if someone had been with me, but also different.

Female solitude is weighted with a particular power in literature. In the absence of her daughters, Ferrante's Leda feels light, she works how and when she wants, she changes her eating habits and begins to listen to music again. She is being returned to something vital, allowed to live and think at the proper speed, at a slower, looser pace, with fewer distractions, and this transforms her mentally and physically. She becomes stronger, younger almost.

So too in *Lolly Willowes,* where Laura, the spinster aunt also known as Lolly, wants more than anything to leave her brother's house in order to be alone. Before she breaks free and moves to Great Mop, she often imagines herself in a

place like it, her daydreams so lucid they resemble halluci-
nations. Once she has arrived and settled in her new home,
she experiences, like Leda, an intense relief. Wandering into
a meadow of blooming cowslips, she kneels to smell their
fragrance. For a moment she is weighed down by her past
unhappiness, and then it is lifted: "It was all gone, it could
never be again, and never had been." I keep thinking and
writing about both *The Lost Daughter* and *Lolly Willowes,*
and in that way the novels have become part of my inner life,
which is also always a part of one's solitude.

To be in favor of solitude is not to be against community
or friendship or love. It's not that being alone is better, just
that without the experience of it we block ourselves from
discovering something enormously beneficial, perhaps even
vital, to selfhood. Who are you when you are not a friend,
a partner, a lover, a sibling, a parent, a child? When no one
is with you, what do you do, and do you do it differently
than if someone was there? It's hard to see someone fully
when another person is always attached to them. More im-
portantly, it's hard for us to see our own selves if we're not
ever alone.

To write, to do any kind of work well, I believe we must at least have a solitude of mind, a solitude of seeing. Of course there are those who collaborate, but even then there must be moments of retreat. We retreat to read. We retreat to think. And so often that thinking can be blotted out by someone else's presence. Dorothea in George Eliot's *Middlemarch* does her deepest and finest thinking when she is alone, not when she is with Casaubon. In Samatar's "Olimpia's Ghost," Gisela is alone too when she writes her brilliant and expressive letters, and she is alone when she dreams. There is life that surrounds each one of us that no one else should enter, lest they drive it off.

Now, I am married, and often with my husband, though we are careful about giving each other space to be alone. On a trip a couple of years ago, Amar and I flew from where we live in Los Angeles to Rome, landing there at night. After dropping our luggage at the guesthouse where we were staying, we wandered nearby, looking for a place to eat. We saw the Colosseum standing in darkness, with no one nearby, and then we sat outside at a restaurant, waiting for our meal, experiencing our first moments of Rome together. I felt a similar euphoria as I had my first night in Beijing, but now the relationship was between my husband and me and Rome, or between the two of us while in Rome. It was not just a relationship between me and Rome, or between him and Rome, in the way it would have been if we had each been traveling on our own.

Maybe we would have felt our separate relationships to the city more acutely if our marriage had been ending, like Katherine and Alexander Joyce's marriage seems to be in Roberto Rossellini's film *Journey to Italy*. Katherine, played by Ingrid Bergman, sees most of Naples by herself, in scenes that are both quiet and disquieting. She is in a very particular solitude there: she visits the tourist attractions in the company of a tour guide, a person who offers her no real connection. When other tourists are present, she remains separate from them, watching them solemnly from an emotional distance.

My husband has had to be away a lot for the last couple of years, so while I've been writing these words about solitude, I've often been alone. Like Leda, the solitude has returned me to something. I feel more desirous when I am alone— mostly for my husband, but also for life, for experience, like

I was when I was younger. I listen to music more intently. It seems to mean more. It is its own kind of euphoria, its own kind of peace. Of course, each time my husband leaves, I know he'll return. If he weren't coming back, my time alone would mean something different.

If I'm honest, I don't want solitude in the absolute way that Lolly wants it. I sometimes get bored of myself, and I quickly miss spending "together alone" time, when you can be with another person quietly, doing your own thing in the same space. I have always liked this kind of intimacy, and my husband and I are good at it: it means a different kind of peace when he is here with me. It is not pure solitude, but I am not, it turns out, a purist. The art of being alone, for many of us, is best appreciated within its limits. Even Leda eventually begins to break down when left to her own devices for too long. Her isolation gives her tranquility, but it also allows her past to come swinging in, some of it violent.

Perhaps solitude is a practice as much as an instinct, its pleasures very much contextual. Sometimes being alone is terrible. I don't ever want to feel as lonely as I did fifteen years ago in Chicago after many of my friends had moved away, when I went to the bathroom at a party and thought, when you go back out, none of the people you love will be there, as they had been at parties past. Equally, I do not want the sharp isolation that comes from proximity to uncaring strangers, or to those who have become unhappily like strangers. As Rossellini's Katherine says to her husband, "I don't think you're very happy when we're alone"—and Alexander responds, "Are you sure you know when I'm happy?"

What I want is to be like the narrator in Jorge Luis Borges' "Argumentum Ornithologicum," alone with my visions. I want to know I have seen what is only visible when I am by myself, even if I spend a good part of my life with others. I don't want to be locked out.

*

COMING BACK FROM NEAR SLEEP, a painting by Hilma af Klint takes shape in my mind. Pink and black, circles and triangles. I like to see what emerges when drifting into, or out of, sleep. Sometimes I am surprised by it, and sometimes it makes sense. Why did *The Swan, No. 13* flash before me again?

Bhanu Kapil pouring a kettle of hot water over red ice cubes at the ICA. I wasn't there; I didn't see it. But one night, after reading her book *How To Wash a Heart*, the image arrives.

Reading *The Weak Spot* by Lucie Elven, pictures emerged too. The candlelit funicular, framed by fir trees. Walkers' heads over the shrubbery, taking their evening strolls.

Sometimes when I come out of sleep, all that emerges is the image of my phone, or my actual phone.

Sometimes it is only my hand. The hand that wrote this down.

*

WHEN I BEGAN LOOKING AT PAINTINGS of nighttime scenes because I wanted to write about them, I felt immediately comforted. It's probably why I was drawn in the first place to write about darkness, but I wasn't expecting to be soothed so quickly. It was a nice evening, going through different representations of dusk and twilight and gloom: two figures moving against a windy blackness; a dark Yosemite; Faust and Mephistopheles riding horses through a witches' Sabbath; a summer night in Arizona. While I looked at these images, the darkness surrounded me as well, outside of my house.

Later, when I told a friend about this comforting quality, he asked if I had read Italo Calvino's *Six Memos for the Next Millennium* (I had; it's one of my favorites). In "Exactitude" is a passage that speaks to something like this, to why lights in a dark city are pleasurable, and why not being able to see everything is pleasing too. At night we "walk abroad," Calvino says, "using the imagination." A walk in the afternoon offers its own kind of satisfaction, a sense of expansiveness and of health, but in the darkness is mystery, the great unknown. So I kept looking into the darkness, and I kept thinking about why else the night might be soothing, especially given that it is associated with so many negative connotations—crime, violence, and hauntings.

It's not that all of my experiences in the dark have been good. One night recently I woke to an explosion that I quickly learned had been a tire blowing up. Someone had set a car on fire in the middle of the street in front of our house. Because our street is narrow and winding, the car was close to us. I was afraid our olive tree would catch on fire, and then our house, or that the whole car would explode, killing us. Most of the earthquakes I've experienced have been at night, almost always when I am in bed, reading or sleeping. And not long before the pandemic was upon us, we woke to our fire alarm and its recorded female voice that announces, anxiously, "Emergency!" I immediately thought something terrible was happening, some kind of natural disaster. Probably because I was disoriented, my mind went to this general idea of emergency instead of to the specific possibility of a fire, and it took me several hours to come down from this, even after it was clear nothing was actually happening, not even a fire. Now it seems like an announcement of the year that was to come, a gateway. A different kind of disaster, but a disaster nonetheless. This is not darkness that soothes. Or a darkness of excitement. Still, I believe in those aspects of darkness too.

Several years ago at LACMA in Los Angeles, I saw Christian Marclay's *The Clock,* a twenty-four hour montage of film clips, in which each clip features a clock that marks that minute of the day. I was in the theater from 10:30 PM to 12:30 AM, and was fascinated by the juxtaposition of scenes of people going to bed with scenes of them getting ready to go out, or already out and creeping around a building. At night, as some people wind down, others are winding up. Some to sleep and others into some seedy or terrifying drama enacted outside of the house, or at least the movies would have us believe this. It's no wonder there's a sense of freedom at night, all of that going to sleep, leaving space for the people who are still awake. And maybe it's no wonder there's a sense of tranquility, as rest is restorative, or should be, and most of us rest at night. But even sleep itself—dreaming—holds that juxtaposition. We might burrow into our comfortable blankets and pillows only to head into a nightmare. Even in sleep, some part of us remains active.

In Virginia Woolf's *The Waves*, Jinny knows and understands this space of one thing closing down while another is opening up, for she is going to a concert, wearing silk stockings and a cold necklace, when others have settled in for the night. In her fine clothes, she is sitting in a concert hall waiting for the fiddlers to take up their bows:

"How strange," said Jinny, "that people should sleep, that people should put out the lights and go up stairs. They have taken off their dresses, they have put on white night-gowns ... there is a line of chimney-pots against the sky; and a street lamp or two burning, as lamps burn when nobody needs them ... the day is over. A few policemen stand at the corners. Yet night is beginning. I feel myself shining in the dark."

Woolf writes so well of this contrast. Night begins, and with it, a quiet descends, and so does a kind of movement.

My walks are almost always at dusk, up and down the hills of my neighborhood, and though I like them at other times of the day too, for me those other walks are not as pleasurable. As the light in the sky dims, lights come on in the houses, and the lives of the people inside the houses seem more interesting then, heightened, as though each house is a stage, the lights illuminating a scene of domesticity. My life feels heightened too, and I appreciate the gentleness of the coming evening. Once, when I was going through a depression, the sunny blaring days were unbearable, and it was only as the sun started to go down that I found relief. I felt so much better at night, closer to the good things I was still sometimes capable of feeling. Think of how nice a desert is in the evening, when even a cactus can look soft.

I think about the darkness in which A and Macedonio are suspended in my favorite Borges story, "A Dialog About a Dialog." Having failed to turn on the lamp as night comes on, they talk about immortality without being able to see each other, "La Cumparsita" carrying on in the background, a song A finds infinitely annoying. He plays with Macedonio's pocketknife and ruminates on suicide, on the soul. A conversation in the dark is intimate; it can lull you, when you can't see another's face or body. Sometimes it is good to let faces and bodies go. Your voices take center stage, consequential in a way they might not be in the light.

In the etching *Conversation at Night* by Théophile-Alexandre Steinlen (1898), darkness is a presence, the heavy black lines creating a night that is deep and impenetrable. Only the woman in the etching is lit and visible, and not completely; much of her is still in shadow. The two men she is speaking with, turned away from the viewer, are more like silhouettes than figures. The piece is literally shrouded in mystery. I wonder what the three of them are talking about. Has the woman stepped outside of her house for a moment to have this curious conversation? Is that why she wears only a dress while the men wear coats and hats? It must be cold. And late. Everyone else must be in bed. But Steinlen didn't want to tell us these things; in this particular darkness, as in any, we must use our imaginations, as Calvino said.

Depending on the time of the year, of course, an hour can be completely light or completely dark. Six o'clock is an hour that holds so much potential. Today it is October, so six o'clock is still light, but in another month it won't be. Most people dislike losing daylight hours, which is understandable, but I like a dark six o'clock as much as I like a bright one. I like the cycles of the year. From Toni Morrison's *Beloved*: "Time came when the lamps had to be lit early because night arrived sooner and sooner. Sethe was leaving for work in the dark; Paul D was walking home in it. On one such evening dark and cool, Sethe cut a rutabaga into four pieces and left them stewing."

Maybe we get closer to something in the dark, or maybe it's the opposite, which is why a stove is so nice at night, and sharing a meal, those points of warmth and light that naturally draw things together. Compared to dinner, lunch can be so boring, without the same kind of depth. In Morrison's novel, as the days grow shorter, Beloved begins to haunt Sethe's household more intensely, and relationships quicken. Everyone and everything in that household draws closer and closer: pain and love, tragedy and healing, the past and the future. Their house with its lights becomes a stage, and the outside that gradually darkens is where the reader sits.

I've never been able to understand people, like my husband, who don't care about lighting, who are immune to harsh overhead lights. It's especially awful in a bedroom, when you are trying to read at night. It isn't conducive to winding down, and it flattens the imagination. In his essay "In Praise of Shadows," Junichiro Tanizaki talks at length about the beauty of darkness: in a house, a meal, the theater. For a long time after electricity had been introduced in Japan, the Bunraku puppet theater continued to light its performances with lamplight, which Tanizaki imagines must have been much more expressive than modern lighting. He says, "a chill comes over me when I think of the uncanny beauty the puppet theater must once have had." But it's when Tanizaki talks about food that I am even more convinced of the pleasures of darkness. He writes:

> I was once invited to a tea ceremony where miso was served; and when I saw the muddy, claylike color, quiet in a black lacquer bowl beneath the faint light of a candle, this soup that I usually take without a second thought seemed somehow to acquire a real depth . . .White foods too—white miso, bean curd, fish cake, the white meat of fish—lose much of their beauty in a bright room.

In Lucas Emil Vorsterman's *Backgammon Players* (1630), a relationship between darkness and light is very much present. Here it's the candlelight as much as the shadows that draw us into the scene. The soft light brightens the faces of the people and brings us closer to them. The flames are warm and flickering, showing us life, their shadows appealing in the way they rise suggestively up the walls. A plain daytime scene would not be nearly as mysterious or layered. And it might only be at night that a man would stare so boldly at a young female musician. The light features this boldness, as well as the girl's obliviousness, making all of it significant against a dark backdrop.

A scene of darkness, whether in writing or art or film, allows for a break, and a bit of quiet, like having a small pillow laid over your eyes. Why shouldn't we rest? But it's not just resting, of course. I think it's also a move to the unconscious mind, to what can be understood without thinking, without trying too hard. A way to sit for a moment with what you are experiencing in the work.

Whatever the reason, darkness captivates, holds its own kind of sovereignty, and we need the change from daylight to night and back again. We need to come down from the day. From Kazuo Ishiguro's *A Pale View of Hills*: "Mariko moved across the room toward the window again. She was just tall enough to lean her elbows on the ledge. For a few minutes she looked into the darkness, her face close to the pane. 'I want to go out now.'"

*

THIS AUTUMN I'VE BEEN READING the diaries of Virginia Woolf, mostly before going to bed at night. In addition to not regularly keeping one, I haven't often read writers' diaries, but I like the entries. I like knowing what Woolf was thinking about her books as she wrote them and their reception after they came out, and what she thinks of the other writers of her time. It is satisfying to be in her mind: "What is the right attitude toward criticism? What ought I to feel and say when Miss B. devotes an article in *Scrutiny* to attacking me? She is young, Cambridge, ardent. And she says I'm a very bad writer."

Woolf didn't write in her diary everyday, and many entries are left out, but they span much of her writing life, from 1918 to 1941, up until the month of her death. I'm not finished with the book, so I don't know what those entries in 1941 will be like, and the years leading up to 1941. I am almost afraid to reach them, in the same way I was afraid, when reading my aunt Allison Miner's diaries, to read the entries close to her death, how sad I knew it would feel, and yet with my aunt it was important, a loving accompaniment. Lately I've been wondering about my own death, when it will come, what I will have been writing just before. Crisis makes you think of it. How could it not? Sometimes I worry I won't have the chance to finish the novel I am now writing.

Maybe I've not kept a diary because imagined lives have been more interesting for me to write down than my own. Yet my life comes into my fiction too, and now I am writing of it here, attached to my reading and my writing. Attached to darkness, solitude, the ocean. Attached to fiction.

My aunt's diaries came to me in a large red duffel bag. There are so many of them, of different sizes and styles and colors, beginning in 1966 and ending in 1995. Thirty years of her life. In the early diaries she writes of the segregated beaches of Daytona, where she grew up, where my mother grew up too, and my grandfather. She writes of music, and of wanting to move to New Orleans. She went to high school with the Allman Brothers, singing in a band with them called The Allman Joys. In an entry from around that time, she wrote that she began to keep a journal because she saw that life had mystical qualities.

I wish we'd been closer. I think I was invisible to her; at least that's how it felt when I was growing up. The only time she wrote of me was to express her surprise that I had become a writer, and that she liked what I had written. She says something like: who knew she had it in her! I connect to her through *her* writing. I feel deep admiration for the life she lived, and pride that I was her niece. At the end, I think she was proud of me too.

As the diaries go on, Allison writes of moving to Louisiana, of co-founding the New Orleans Jazz and Heritage Festival, of her marriage and divorce and her children, of her work with musicians like Professor Longhair, whom she managed, of her on-and-off-again relationship with Allen Touissant and her sadness over it, of other affairs and friendships, of her deep feeling of loneliness despite the many people in her life, of her fear of the mental illness that seemed to overtake the women in our family, like it did her mother—my grandmother—who was diagnosed with schizophrenia. She was afraid it would overtake her too. I am sometimes afraid of the same thing. Finally, of cancer, from which she died when she was forty-six, the same age I was when I read her diaries.

Sometimes I feel I should write a book about her life, and my family prods me in that direction, but it's not the kind of writing I normally do. Though I learned something about writing, about diaries, when I read hers. They're compelling, and it was an immersion in that form. Interiority is one of my favorite things to read in fiction—to abide in a narrator's mind if that narrator, that mind, compels me—and when you read a diary you have that, ten fold. A diary is intimate, forthright, immediate.

From one of Woolf's entries in October of 1920: "Here I sit at Richmond, and like a lantern stood in the middle of a field my life goes up in darkness." She's melancholy, but she says that writing helps her not be. It helps me too. I imagine it helped Allison. In another entry Woolf writes of Katherine Mansfield: "She said a good deal about feeling things deeply: also about being pure, which I won't criticize, though of course I very well could. But now, what do I feel about *my* writing—this book, that is, *The Hours*, if that's it's name? One must write from deep feeling, said Dostoevsky. And do I?"

That sense of deep feeling is in her novels, always. *Mrs Dalloway*, *The Waves*, *To the Lighthouse*, *The Voyage Out*, *Night and Day*. When I've read them, I've gotten to feel deeply too.

Here is a sentence from my own diary from February of 2021: "I have never wanted to write something tragic." But what I think I want and what I am urged forward by is not always the same thing. I write to see what is inside my mind. For me, it is often far better, healthier, than recording what I know is already there.

*

IN THE LAST YEAR I'VE BECOME fixated on the idea of authenticity. This is partly because I feel at times I have lost sight of my authentic self, and I want more than anything to come close to it again, or at least to *feel* close to it. For me, authenticity means that how I act and what I say and how I actually feel around others is aligned, that I am connected to myself and to another person at the same time. I want my writing to be authentic too, for every sentence to reach toward honesty and meaning.

In his play *The Maids*, Jean Genet manages to come up to the very edge of authenticity in that nothing is held back, everything is expressed, everything breaks the surface and is free. First performed in Paris in 1947, the play is loosely based on the infamous Papin sisters, who murdered their employer in 1933 in Le Mans, France.

In their roles as maids in the rooms of Madame's high-class apartment, Solange and Claire become unhinged, especially when they are there alone. They are free then to do as they like, and the desire for another reality, and the level to which they pitch that desire, drives them into an electrifying realm of fantasy and performance, in which they take turns playing each other and Madame, and play at cruelty and revenge. It feels as if this is what the end of fantasy looks like, if you follow it as far as it can possibly go. And if the fantasy is as filled with bitterness and rage as the sisters are, then it feels like it will explode.

In this performance, which they call "the ceremony," they can be their most authentic selves, because they are in alignment with their true feelings and desires. They are acknowledging with real honesty how others feel toward them, and reacting honestly to it. Because of this sense of freedom, this reach toward liberty, the play feels oddly clean, satisfying.

But when one sister overpowers the other, an already unsettling situation gets even darker. It doesn't seem that it could. It is painful to hear the insults the sisters hurl at each other. They understand all too well how they are seen by society, with what distaste—disgust, even. Claire yells at Solange: "A vile and odious breed, I loathe them. They're not of the human race. Servants ooze. They're a foul effluvium drifting through our rooms and hallways, seeping into us, entering our mouths, corrupting us."

The play shows us the risks of an expression without limits, of following desire to its breaking point, especially if it has been pushed down by an oppressive system. In this case, class. Genet recognized, as does director Bong Joon-ho in his film *Parasite,* the horror and tragedy of turning that expression inward, or at those who occupy a similar class role, namely as servants to the rich. Both works portray self-harm in brutal ways.

When the maids know Madame will soon be coming home, they rush to put things back in their places, including themselves, slipping back into their "proper" roles. Now they play at being nice to her; now they are false. In their relationship to Madame, they cannot be their authentic selves. Their identities hinge upon their service to her, always. And is Madame false also? When she is nice to them, gives them compliments and clothing, is it real, or is it pity? As the provider of their livelihood, does she think of herself as a savior? Does she ever see them as they actually are? For the introduction to the play, Jean-Paul Sartre wrote: "In like manner, wealthy, cultivated and happy men have, from time to time, 'felt sorry' for Genet, have tried to oblige him. Too late. He has blamed them for loving him for the love of Good, *in spite of* his badness and not for it."

My loss of authenticity is related to change, to how, as I've gotten older, I seem to have become a different person. In a way I have become strange to myself, and so how I am and feel around others has also been destabilized. I have more fears than I had when I was younger; I am more rigid; and there has been a loss too of the freedom I once felt, when the world seemed entirely open, and utterly beautiful. I don't know if I can say that I have been able yet to move meaningfully toward authenticity in my life, but to face this loss with honesty has in itself felt significant. And in my writing I am able to be close to who I am, or at least access parts of myself I thought I had lost. I named one of the characters in my novel after one of the sisters, Solange, not with the intent to rewrite her, but because I was interested in the currents that often remain invisible, that aren't usually acted out as they are in *The Maids*.

My Solange is not Genet's Solange, but she is a maid, to a woman named Vitória who, before marrying her rich husband, was also a cleaner. I wanted my Solange to carry within her the potential of the other Solange, and a dark history of maids throughout time. Solange does not like Vitória; she makes this very clear. Solange keeps herself walled off, protected. But this is a fulltime project, for they must see each other every day, living as they do in the same house.

How often these dynamics have existed, and still exist, in the space of the home, where "Madame" and "Monsieur" lay their heads and sleep, where they sleep with each other, and where "their" servants in other rooms live their own private realities too. Of course these kinds of relationships aren't always bad, but when they are bad, to have to live together, employer and employee, is its own unique condition. Home should be a place of retreat and safety (though we know that's not always so). Above all, a place where you can be yourself. To have to maintain those class roles always, especially if they are enforced with any kind of degradation, is a violation of the sacredness of one's life, and a violence all on its own.

The ceremony Genet's sisters engage in enacts this kind of violation and violence, but it also engenders a sense of intimacy and, again, freedom. It is Madame's apartment, true, but it is *their* stage, and in some ways they are very much at home there. And when Claire and Solange perform the ceremony, they wear Madame's clothes. In *The Maids*, domestic space is political, as it always has the potential to be. Ownership can't permeate all of life, and part of what *The Maids* does best is to push it off, and to push off the oppressive roles class and servitude create.

The end of the play contains an ultimate violence and with it an ultimate sadness. The maids are allowed to be their real selves only through sacrifice, by entering a space no one should ever have to enter. I'm being cryptic, but I don't want to give anything away. As a writer and an artist, Genet wasn't afraid to enter into any of it, and that is part of how he gets close to authenticity. In the play, Solange says in a moment of exhaustion, "Be yourself again. Come on, Claire, be my sister."

*

NOT LONG AGO, WHEN I RE-READ Gladman's *Ana Patova Crosses a Bridge*, a line formed directly from it to her book of prose, *Calamities*, and so I re-read it too. Then the line began to glow.

I don't know if I'll be able to describe the line, but I'll try. The line has to do with drawing, and what is amazing is that Gladman doesn't just describe drawing in each book—she enters the space of it, taking the reader with her. As someone who doesn't draw, I'd never had the chance to enter a drawing space before. In *Calamities*, Gladman calls what she does "writing-drawing," and says that she does it over and over until it becomes her work. She says that when she was writing it, *Ana Patova* moved through her life so cleanly and quickly that afterwards she couldn't feel any trace of it in her body. She couldn't feel physically that she had written it. "Immediately upon finishing it I went straight into drawing, though it was a drawing that was rather like writing, and maybe there, in the drawings, was the record of this book I had made."

So there is a line too from *Ana Patova* directly into drawing. I have always wanted to think that writing can be enough, and maybe it makes me a little sad if it can't be, but for Gladman it isn't. When she is writing-drawing, she doesn't feel lonely in the way she sometimes does when she is only writing. She says, "I drew against a hum in my head that was like happiness."

There is another line, even if it is a little blurry for me. This one goes from *Calamities* to one of Gladman's much earlier books, *A Picture-Feeling*, published in 2005. A book I have read, but because it has been a long time since I checked it out from the library and no longer have it with me, and because I sometimes have a bad memory, I can no longer remember it. In *Calamities*, Gladman writes of the language she is discovering in her writing-drawing process, "I'd learned that to think in this language you had to be patient: you had to say one part, like drawing one side of a cube, then say the next part, like drawing another side, and keep on saying and drawing until eventually you'd made a complex observation and a picture-feeling."

Because I cannot remember the book, that picture-feeling is mysterious, and it's pleasing to imagine Gladman thinking in 2005 about a feeling she would enter with her body, her writing-drawing hand, in 2013 when *Ana Patova Crosses a Bridge* came out, and in 2016 when *Calamities* came out, and in 2017, the year her first book of drawings, *Prose Architectures,* came out, and all of the years in between, the years she wrote and drew those books. Of course, she may have entered a picture-feeling much earlier than I am imagining.

On the last page of *Calamities*, a literal drawn line appears that seems to lead to Gladman's two books of drawings, *Prose Architectures* and *One Long Black Sentence* (indexed by Fred Moten). I wonder what line will come next.

*

AS I WRITE THIS, MY CAT TROUT whines loudly in the kitchen. It's unfortunate to use the word "my" when talking about him, this marker of ownership, yet I do. Trout is direct and bossy about his need for affection; he demands it throughout the day. That is why he is whining now. I understand that I have made him into a pet, a dependent, yet I also understand how he controls me, how I structure my mornings around his needs in a way most people wouldn't. When he reaches the last ten or so pieces of food in his dish, he sits patiently in front of it, until I pick up the pieces by hand and place them on the floor next to his dish. He is striking, the mark between his eyes that looks religious, the mark that runs down his cheek.

I'm taken with Kate Zambreno's attentive and loving writing on her dog Genet in her novel *Drifts*. There is a study of Genet within the novel, with his "Sontag mohawk" and his funny personality. In fact, the novel is dedicated to him. He and the narrator are close, spending hours alone together at home, walking. They sit on the porch in a meditative silence, until Genet hears or sees something at which he cannot resist barking. "Quiet, quiet, I say to Genet, as dogs walk by, which he obeys by ruffing softly yet firmly to himself." Sometimes they listen together, disturbed and sympathetic, to the sounds of a man in pain across the street.

In her days with Genet, writing with him fitfully by her side (there is no window in the study for him to look out of, or he wants to play), the narrator is also thinking of Rilke, of the elderly woman who lives in her neighborhood, of the stray cats. It is a book of interiors and exteriors, of the mind, calm and cluttered, and as a reader it is a pleasure to rest there. She looks at sketches of animals by Albrecht Dürer, where she sees the likeness of Genet and the other animals they encounter on their walks: "I think of the identical feral cats that lurk outside of the new cat house and I begin to see the house and the sidewalks as a dimensional space like one of Dürer's engravings, as if it is the same striped cat that is drawn in different poses." *Drifts* is a study too of these animals, in Dürer's sketches, in her neighborhood. A study of that kind of merging. Of that kind of space.

I hadn't looked at Dürer's sketches and drawings of animals before, not carefully. He did so many, each one precise and charming. My favorite is of a wild sow, with its stripes and pointed ears, its friendly eyes and snout (I can picture it eating), its compact body, a tail that looks like it belongs to a much smaller animal.

Trout does not accept a life spent entirely indoors, nor do I think he should, even though there are coyotes where we live. We are both neurotic, and the coyotes make us more so. For a year, they were here all the time. They made a den down the hill from us, and at dusk their yips and howls were loud and near. That loudness and nearness astonished me. I saw a coyote several times each day, at any hour, sometimes two running down the street together, or up the hill toward our house.

I began to think they were trolling me, I saw them so often, eventually even in my dreams. Once, when I was away for work for a couple of days, I saw one immediately upon returning. There the coyote sat in our driveway, right in the spot where my car was meant to be. The coyotes made their own dimensional space around our house. I became obsessed with them, reading as much about them as I could. I learned that what sounds like ten coyotes is usually more like two or three, and once I actually got to see this play out. Standing on the deck at dusk, I watched two coyotes at the bottom of the hill raise their heads and yip frenetically, while a coyote I couldn't see yipped in the distance. They were calling out to each other, communicating their locations, and eventually the coyote in the distance made its way to the other two and there the three of them called out together, so much louder and more chaotic than I ever would have thought three coyotes could be. I feel lucky to have seen this, and I admire them greatly. I worry about how thin they are, feel sad if I see one limping or with open wounds on its back. They are beautiful animals.

When they were here, I tried to keep Trout inside, but he rebelled, sprayed inside the house, and once when I myself was on the toilet, jumped on my lap, turned around, and sprayed *me*. Due to the stress of staying inside, he had developed an inflamed bladder, a condition that could have killed him as quickly as any coyote would. I let him out again, then, but in a controlled and neurotic way, checking on him constantly. Now I was afraid I was going to get sick. I'm positive my neighbors thought I was crazy; how often I appeared outside, looking all around the house, down the street. Somehow we survived that time, but the coyotes could build a den at the bottom of the hill again at any time. They change homes and circuits every so often, to throw off any would-be predators, and because their dens become infested with fleas.

In Sigrid Nunez's *The Friend,* the relationship between the narrator and her dog is as profound as any human relationship might be. I feel that Apollo is the friend the title references, but it must be the human friend instead, the one who has committed suicide and is now gone. The one who has left Apollo behind. And yet, a dog is on the cover of the book, not a man.

The narrator's apartment building doesn't allow animals, but she sneaks Apollo in, a Great Dane, not easy to hide, which almost gets her evicted. He is an older dog, has arthritis, has lost most of his energy, and on top of that is depressed. He must miss the man he lived with before. They miss him together. But still he is regal, even when he stops in the middle of a walk, refusing to go on. People gasp on the street when they see how majestic he is.

Apollo doesn't seem interested in his new owner at first, and she feels her own distance from him. In the daytime he ignores her in the apartment and sleeps facing the wall. He takes over her bed, once even growling at her when she tries to get him to come down. For a while she lets him have the bed, sleeping on an air mattress instead. But one night she awakens to Apollo snuffling her head, digging his nose into her neck, placing his giant paw on her chest. In time, she comes to love him deeply, but he is already old; their time together is limited. She thinks, "That disaster has been averted, that we are spared separation or eviction—I'm sorry, but it's not enough. Now I am like the Fisherman's wife: I want more. And not just another summer, or two or three or four. I want Apollo to live as long as I do."

There's a painting I like by Andrew Wyeth called *Wild Dog* (1959), in which a black dog is running through the snow, each foot sunk into it. You can't see the dog's face. The dog is looking at something out of frame, distracted, its ears pricked up. I love the dog's posture, its back legs moving toward its front legs, low to the ground. A slow careful run, aware of its surroundings. I wonder where it lives, if it sleeps in a den, if it ever runs with a pack. A dog running has always been one of my favorite things to see. Also a horse.

Our other cat, Albertine, bullies Trout. Sweet to us, she is terrible to him. She contributes to his desire to go outside beyond the protective fence, chasing him out of the courtyard she has claimed as her territory, off of cat beds, away from the food dishes. Right now she is curled up next to me, her paw on my arm, her whiskers twitching. The softness of Albertine, who catches toy mice in her two front paws like a star pitcher or goalie. She is athletic in her playing. At night in the summer, I keep the glass patio door open in our bedroom and put one of her two cat beds (since she has claimed both) in front of the screen, where she stays riveted much of the night, staring into the dark courtyard that is visited by some other kind of animal we hear but never see. Can Albertine?

One night I heard loud licking sounds, a possum eating loquats from our tree, and I shot a video of it on my phone, the dark courtyard, the slurping sounds. When the coyotes had their den here, I stood on our back deck and recorded their loud yipping in the same way, the darkness of the hillside next to us.

*

IN *THE FROZEN THAMES*, HELEN HUMPHREYS writes of that river forty times to imagine the years it has frozen solid. The first freezing in the book takes place in 1142, the last in 1895. The words "vignette" and "episode" appear in the jacket copy as a way to describe the form of each story, but to me each piece is also a rendering, of the Thames, of freezing. I like "rendering" partly because of its relationship to drawing, but also, Humphreys brings a representation of the river to life again and again. She helps us to see it in 1506. In 1768. Quick but rich and lively portraits of the river in those cold winters, those bitter years. Frost fairs, starving, lovers meeting on the ice during an epidemic.

My favorite moment in the book comes in the very first freezing. Matilda, the rightful queen of England, is trapped inside her castle by her cousin Stephen. It has been like this for three months. When she finally makes her escape, it is during a deep snow. "Big, lacy flakes that swim down out of the darkness decorate the shoulders of the Queen's maid. 'Ma'am,' says Jane. 'The snow is the same colour as your nightshirt.'" So Matilda and three of her men wear nightshirts for their crossing; they wear white bonnets. Out on the river, a sentry seems to notice their passing, but instead of stopping them he blesses himself. Humphreys writes: "he must have thought that they were ghosts." I like imagining this crossing, but not for its adventure. It's the image I love, Matilda and her knights moving nearly invisibly through a blizzard, the river a new kind of passageway, so frozen even a fire can be lit upon it. A portrait of escape.

Since I live in Los Angeles, I am in a city where it doesn't snow, but I still want a feeling of winter, even if I don't want to live in it, exactly. There are days each year when I can drive up the Angeles Crest and walk there in the snow, and days when I can see it from my front porch on the peaks of the San Gabriel mountains, but the only other way to have a feeling of winter is to see an image of it in a painting or movie, or through setting in a story or a novel, to read it, and sometimes to write it. I just finished reading *Winter* by Adam Gopnik. In his chapter "Romantic Winter," he writes of that season as a lure for the Romantic imagination, for the way "it makes dead forms look as nice as living ones." Like hoarfrost on the windowpanes and the falling snow, mimicking flowers. I'd never thought of it in that way, though now it seems obvious. Snow and ice rising from their cold chambers, not to haunt, but to conjure a false sense of newness. I myself have a romantic imagination; I fall victim to that trap. I have always carried warmth into the cold.

Tove Jansson's novel *The True Deceiver* is literally half snow: the narrative would be so different without it. The snow is part of what makes the relationship between Katri Kling and Anna Aemelin so uneasy, and it adds to the uneasiness in Katri herself.

> Inside the snow banks were deep, narrow tunnels where the children had dug hideouts for themselves during thaws. And outside stood their snowmen, snowhorses, formless shapes with teeth and eyes of bits of tin and coal. When the next hard freeze came, they poured water over these sculptures so they'd harden to ice. One day Katri paused before one of these images and saw that it was a likeness of herself.

A portrait of Katri, in ice. I feel as though I were looking at it. Imagine finding your likeness in that way. Are you alive or are you dead? What has been captured, there in the ice?

How strange and sometimes demonic the faces of babies and children in early portrait paintings. How stern the adults. Sometimes they soften, but they rarely smile. Why do we smile now? In Italy, when I looked at paintings at the Uffizi Gallery in Florence, the figure with the softest expression on her face was *Portia,* wife of Brutus, painted by Bartolomeo della Porta (1495), and she has just helped murder Julius Caesar. I suppose della Porta wanted to portray some crucial aspect of the situation in Portia's face. Does it relax her to think of the deed done, to think of Julius Caesar now gone? Like Wyeth's black dog, she isn't looking at the viewer, and points to someone, or something, we can't see. After her husband commits suicide, she kills herself too by swallowing hot coals, pictured at the bottom of the painting. Maybe it's the coal to which she's pointing or looking, knowing what comes next. Regardless, she seems to be at peace.

In *Portrait of Galeazzo Maria Sforza*, painted by Piero del Pollaiolo (1471) to commemorate the ruler of Milan's visit to Florence, Galeazzo's expression is grimmer than Portia's, even though all she is doing is visiting. She too appears to point at someone or something we can't see, while clutching an unidentifiable object in her hand. Why are figures in paintings so often gesturing to what's out of view? To remind us of the beyond, I suppose. Both paintings retain their mystery.

Here is another mystery, from Fleur Jaeggy's "Portrait of an Unknown Woman" in *I Am the Brother of XX*: "Sometimes before a portrait something imperious and hidden, a detail, captures our attention. Does not let the gaze wander. When I abandon it, by an act of will, and resume my rounds in the halls of the museum, I am compelled to go back." How can a detail be urgent and at the same time concealed? In fiction, what does that look like? And how do we bring the reader back to it? Perhaps it never leaves us, is part of the visual impression of what we've read, the narrative unfolding in pictures running parallel to its unfolding through events. An impression can be just as important as meaning.

One of the things I like about portraiture in painting and drawing and photography is that it allows for a suspension in one moment, one figure, and I think that in fiction, if readers are patient enough for it, description can get close to this too. Like watching a snowstorm from inside a house. Then you go out finally, into the snow. The action is restored. Reading *The True Deceiver*, I like experiencing those scenes of winter, as long as they are, staying on as winter itself does, and now that it's been a while since I've read that novel, it's those images of snow and ice that stay with me as much as the strange things the characters say to each other, or the moments when something is very palpably left unsaid.

In Tisa Bryant's *Unexplained Presence* a continuum comes into being, or else a light is shone on connections already present between people (or characters) who existed throughout time (or in art or film or literary history) but never knew each other, or even knew to know each other. Bryant looks at and writes into films, novels, and paintings, "cataloguing the ways blackness persists in culture: as curio, as enabler, as counter-example, as temptation, as nightmare." One of my favorite pieces is "The Problem of Dido," which begins: "Somewhere, in the Continuum of our now, two girls sit for a portrait on their uncle's massive Kenwood estate." Bryant is conjuring the famous portrait of Dido Elizabeth Belle and her white cousin, Lady Elizabeth Murray, painted by David Martin in 1779. Dido, not even fully named in the title of the portrait, the daughter of Sir John Lindsay of the Royal Navy and Maria Belle, the latter of whom is thought to have been a slave in the West Indies, was raised by her great uncle William Murray during the case of the *Zong* trial over which he presided as Chief Justice of England.

Now there is a film of Dido's life called *Belle*, but before that, Bryant imagined the moment of that portrait, and then moved forward from it to imagine Dido's life, what she might have encountered and thought, bringing it to touch the life and story of Ourika, also raised by a white family, in France around 1786, and destroyed by that experience. Bryant's form of ekphrasis is the most affecting I know, to not only describe a painting, but to animate it in this way, to enter history, including art history, to bring to light that continuum of which she writes.

What are we seeing when we look at a portrait? When we read it? Traditionally, we think of the way a person or character looks, has arranged themself for the artist or photographer, the writer, but if the person or character remains unarranged? That is a portrait too. Can we envision thoughts, thinking? In *Portraits in Fiction*, A.S. Byatt writes that portraits in novels and stories may be of things the reader can't see, like energy, or subtle change, or even great upheaval. It makes me think about the ways in which we can understand how a character looks based not on a physical description, but on how other characters react to their presence. Francine Prose talks about this in her book *Reading Like a Writer* when she writes of Heinrich von Kleist's *The Marquise of O,* a novella whose characters are never given physical descriptions, and yet, Prose says, we are able to form pictures of them all the same.

As a writer, I feel I am always negotiating that: when to give something explicitly to the reader and when to hold back, or when to give just a little of it so that it can be sensed rather than simply seen. There is great value in what can be sensed. And in a way, one of the things that allows fiction its sense of possibility and freedom is this choice of what to make visible. Like thinking and talking; what remains in the mind and what actually gets said. What is it that should be written down? What should be drawn or painted? Which details are the ones that will illuminate the text, making it memorable?

Byatt goes on to say in *Portraits in Fiction* that Honoré de Balzac sometimes used real paintings to describe the characters in his work, as in his short story "The Unknown Masterpiece." In describing a young Poussin seeing the old master Frenhofer for the first time, Balzac wrote of Frenhofer, "You could have said it was a picture by Rembrandt proceeding silently, without a frame, through the darkened atmosphere." Byatt adds: "Balzac's description details those notes we linger over in a Rembrandt portrait—and then he turns the whole thing ghostly by making it live."

He turns the whole thing ghostly by making it live. The thought of what is beyond the frame of a painting has always been appealing to me, as appealing, I imagine, as the figure in the frame looking out at their world, but so is bringing to life a character or likeness of a person who is usually sitting still. What will they do when they finally get up? Where will they go? Of course that would be ghostly, and in many ways so is ekphrasis itself, giving movement to someone or something that was supposed to remain a single image. Letting the portrait walk. The living form, always in relation to the dead one. The ice sculpture of Katri. And the romantic imagination, always there to see it.

In Tarjei Vesaas's beautiful and heartbreaking novel *The Ice Palace*, it's the reverse. After bonding intensely with eleven-year-old Siss the night before, eleven-year-old Unn goes by herself the next morning to see an enormous frozen waterfall in the middle of a forest and never comes back from exploring its labyrinthine chambers. The ice palace is sublime, and Unn is mesmerized by it until she finally becomes trapped. As Gopnik reminds us in *Winter*: "ice is capable of making forms, by accident, that are Gothic in their intricate tracery—a typical hallucination of the era, when the bergs and glaciers were constantly seen as passing ships, castles, cathedrals." This is deadly winter, what it might be like for one's own movements to become still.

*

FINISHED NDIAYE'S *ALL MY FRIENDS*. Such a strange book. What is it in her fiction that draws me? Her imagination is unbelievable. And her humor. She certainly goes all the way in and then out the other side. That is the side one reads.

I graze at my writing. I want to withdraw into it, but of course I also want to live. Mostly I want to go too far, but with a light touch. NDiaye does that.

On lightness, Calvino says this: "I have tried to remove weight, sometimes from people, sometimes from heavenly

bodies, sometimes from cities; above all I have tried to remove weight from the structure of stories and from language."

*

IN *THE RAVISHING OF LOL STEIN*, a friend is someone named
Tatiana who witnesses you being abandoned for another
woman by your fiancé at a ball, and with whom you sym-
bolically, and in a twisted way, recreate and perform this
rejection, years after it first occurred. In the novel *Blue
Eyes, Black Hair*, also by Duras, the two main characters
aren't friends, but they do immerse themselves in a strange
kind of intimacy. The book is about a man and a woman
who spend time together, but in a way that most of us don't
spend time. He's not attracted to women, but he pays her
to lie naked in a room with him night after night, repulsed
by her because she's female. She doesn't seem to care; this
relationship enlivens her somehow. "It suits her very well,
what she's going through with him now. She wonders what

she would have done instead if they hadn't met in the café. It's here in this room that she's had her real summer, her experience, her encounter with hatred of her own sex, and of her body, and of her life."

If you are my friend, please don't be worried that I will expect things like this from you. I am simply in awe of the many ways characters, and people, know each other, the many ways they are close, or distant, and stay in each other's lives. I am fascinated by this.

Sometimes friends meet each other after a long period of loneliness, which is a miraculous thing, to find someone and be found after all that time alone. Each has already gotten to know their own self, maybe too well. Too much time alone is just as risky as not enough, for it allows us to sink into our cyclical patterns of thought and narrative. We need someone to hold up a mirror so we can see who we are when we are taken outside of our heads. We need to hear others' thoughts too. Below is a passage from *Jane Eyre* by Charlotte Brontë, one of my favorite scenes in literature, in which a young Jane has just been sent away to boarding school by her mean and ungenerous aunt, and will soon develop an affection for the young Helen Burns. Jane is a character who epitomizes aloneness, has had to endure outright hostility from her extended family, but her inner life has grown rich, which we see here.

> I wandered as usual among the forms and tables and laughing groups without a companion, yet not feeling lonely: when I passed the windows I now and then lifted a blind and looked out; it snowed fast, a drift was already forming against the lower panes; putting my ear close to the window, I could distinguish from the gleeful tumult within, the disconsolate moan of the wind outside. Probably, if I had lately left a good home and kind parents, this would have been the hour when I should most keenly have regretted the separation: that wind would then have saddened my heart; this obscure chaos would have disturbed my peace: as it was, I derived from both a strange excitement, and reckless and feverish, I wished the wind to howl more wildly, the gloom to deepen to darkness, and the confusion to rise to clamour. Jumping over forms, and creeping under tables, I made my way to one of the fire-places; there, kneeling by the high wire fender, I found

Burns, absorbed, silent, abstracted from all round by the companionship of a book, which she read by the dim glare of the embers.

What I like most about this passage and the way it speaks to friendship is how Jane finds Burns in the midst of her excited fever, and in the midst of connecting to her own self, to life. When confusion gives rise to "clamour" what is better than a friend to explore that with? There are things that can be pitched even higher through friendship than they could be alone.

One of the closest companions I've ever had was a petite prince of a cat named Ingmar. I got him from the Humane Society the week after moving into my first apartment in Columbus, Ohio when I was twenty. We lived with one of my boyfriends, and when it was time to go to bed, Ingmar would wait in the corner of the bedroom until I turned away from my boyfriend, and then he would walk over to the bed, paw at the covers, and I would let him crawl in.

It's possible to be very close to animals, yet human/animal relationships are as complicated as human/human ones. In her book *Creaturely Poetics*, Anat Pick talks about the human/animal relationship through a lens of surface and vulnerability. Thinking through the writing of John Berger and Laura Mulvey, she writes that animals are seen not as they really are, but as cartoons, toys, pets, and as exhibits at the zoo. Instead of sentient beings with their own desires, they have become, as Mulvey described it, "bearers of the human look." We represent them as they aren't in order to make them what we wish them to be, and this is the exact opposite of friendship, of connection—a relationship built on fantasy. This gives us power over them, which separates instead of brings us closer.

Berger reminds us that even with all this observation on our part, animals observe us too. Ingmar used to watch me all the time, staring into my eyes, never flinching as humans do. What do animals see when they look at us? Who are we, to them? I've often thought of the incredible trust that animals—domesticated ones—have placed in us throughout time—humans, who have been kind and also very unkind, who have the potential to love or to kill them. This is one sort of terrible vulnerability. But that's true of human-to-human relationships too, loving or killing. Or just loving and harming, which happens all the time, as we are imperfect beings, and this too is part of the continuum.

On her old blog *Was Jack Kerouac a Punjabi?*, Bhanu Kapil once spoke of her friendship with Melissa Buzzeo, saying that, "Melissa is a friend whose name is written on my heart. I would not be surprised if I die soon! My heart is quite scarred with the names of my friends!!!!! I chose, in this life, to love my friends as deeply and with as much loyalty as if we shared an ethnic bond." This is the most beautiful thing I've ever heard anyone say about a friend, about friendship. I've sometimes thought that if I died suddenly it would be okay, because I've already had such deeply perfect company in this life, more than any one person deserves. I'm grateful for it, and I carry it with me always.

I love the resiliency of friendship, the way you can lose a friend and then find each other again one or five or ten years later. I'm interested in friendships that have over time become awkward, most likely because you have both changed, and you are not as close as you once were, but you refuse to give up. You soldier on, sisters now, or brother and sister, or brothers. I'm an only child, so I'm not quite sure if this comparison is an apt one, but it makes sense to me. You become family. And maybe later you will emerge into something else. Something not better but different.

I am thinking now of a particular time in my life, in Chicago, when I began to meet the people who would become some of the best friends I had ever known. With a few, we announced how much we liked each other before we had spent much time together. This made me nervous. What if when we did spend time it didn't go well? What if one of us got bored? But we didn't get bored, or at least if we ever got bored we didn't mind it. We went on to become people who knew each other, who liked each other as much as we had from the beginning. Some of these friendships expanded beyond the traditional borders, without altering the original feeling they had held. It was one of the few times I've experienced intimacy without grasping.

In the last few years, I've noticed something of a fascination with toxic female friendships in literature. If you Google that topic, you will find a number of lists of novels that feature toxic female friendships. Women, especially, seem interested in them, as something they want to read, and it seems to be part of the reason Ferrante's Neapolitan novels have gained such popularity. I love the novels too, as well as Elena and Lila, but not for their friendship, necessarily, which never seems to me completely close, though I like that it encompasses their entire lives, receding and then becoming stronger again over and over throughout time. I understand difficulty in a friendship, and falling out, but not the idea of the "frenemy." I am not interested at all in competitiveness between women, in toxic female friendships as a literary topic. Maybe I am refusing something in the continuum, but I'm not sure it belongs on the continuum at all. I think it is something different, an internalized patriarchy.

Ironically, I had a falling out (our second) with a good friend a year after giving her *My Brilliant Friend*, the first of the four novels, as a gift. I thought she would like them, and she did, but they brought up a lot for her, which I hadn't anticipated, though maybe I should have. After reading all four, she sent me a long email that concluded with something along the lines of: don't give me a book like Elena Ferrante's and expect to get a smiley face in return. I still love this friend, think of her as brilliant, in fact (she does not think of me as brilliant in return, which she made clear in her email), and in a way she reminds me of Ferrante's female characters: intense and probing, intelligent, with episodes of unrefinement and a bluntness that can become absolutely harsh.

What do I do when my friendships turn "bad," I who pride myself on the deep, loving friendships I have? Because this is a continuum we are talking about, maybe it is inevitable that some friends will feel badly toward each other in the end, or become too changed to go on. The distance can't be crossed anymore; it is too great. And the memory of your former closeness will be comforting, or you will feel grief. Anything is possible. What does it mean to know someone? What does it mean to be close, or to be distant? And is there a part of you that can still be close in the midst of distance?

*

WRITE INTO THE WINTER, AND THE SUMMER, and autumn, and spring. Write into the snow and flowers and the wreaths and the wallpaper. Write into the painting and the flame of the long candle. Write into your own mind, turning and turning it. Write into *L'Homme Assis Dans Le Couloir*. Write into the floor, the wide planks of the mind. Write into the circular gravel driveway that brings your characters to you, that brings them to life. Write into the buffalo and the hare and the dog. Write into the bulb with a miniature pasture painted onto it that hangs on the tree. The bulb of grass outside the house. The buckwheat that is growing in the evening. Write into your eyes. The lamp that sits on the table in the evening. You can see it in the mirror. A pale shade of pink. Write into falling snow, falling rain, falling leaves. Write into the dark stove. A bird of paradise. Write into the ceiling and the scalloped edge. Write into a drawing of a necklace. People praying in church. Write into the cane. The needle and the cloth. Into the times you were unhappy. Write into the fuchsia and black dress. The neckline is low. The cats, curled into little balls on the bed. The endless study. Write into your laziness. Write into the dark lines of the room. Write into the movie you watched. Write into the tall ceilings. The others who were in the room. This tree that is itself in the shape of a ball. Into the shapes around it. Write into the holiday. Into the hedges that line the walk.

*

ON MY LAPTOP ARE JPGS OF PAINTINGS of women reading books. One is lying in the sand surrounded by grass, another is sitting at a table. I dragged them there from the Internet, not quite knowing why I was doing it. But now I realize something in me relaxes when I look at them. The women are all in repose, sitting or lying down. Lost in what they are reading, deep in concentration. They look healthy. When we are that relaxed, we are healthy. In one of my favorites, *The Travelling Companions* (1862), by Augustus Leopold Egg, two girls who look like sisters and are dressed exactly alike sit on opposite sides of their train compartment, opposite sides of the composition. There is an almost perfect symmetry between them, their hats resting in their laps in exactly the same manner, their silk dresses that, when they meet in the middle of the compartment, look as if they are different folds of the same piece of cloth. One girl sleeps while the other reads. Each is resting in her own way. All of us need this kind of rest.

When we read novels or short stories we're supposed to want tension and conflict, at least that's what we're often told, but I don't care about conflict in fiction any more than the other elements that might appear there. It's often narrative voice to which I'm drawn, for the way it sounds, for its interiority, and the way the reader can follow it through a narrative, for the way it can excite or unsettle or soothe. To read relaxation should be boring, for what are we paying attention to when we encounter it? How is it driving the story forward? Something is always supposed to be driving another thing forward in some way.

There is so much pleasure in *Lolly Willowes*, as when Laura, finally, at age forty-seven, goes toward her true nature for the first time: she becomes a witch, or she becomes *herself* as a witch. There is something calming about that, to give up a charade of what you are supposed to be, of what you have tried, unsuccessfully, to be your whole life; to take off those obligations, setting them down beside you; to move to the country, in touch with the supernatural. The passage in which this transformation begins is on page seventy-eight. The book has already shown Laura living one kind of life, in which what she wants she gets only in small doses. She wants nature and wildness, and in Apsley Terrace, where she lives with her brother and his family, she surrounds herself with flowers, every winter she fills her room with them, but that isn't enough. It's that shop that's "half florist and half green grocer" that leads Laura to what will be her new home, her new existence. She's deeply pleased by everything in the shop: the flowers and the vegetables, the bottled fruit. She begins to feel a longing, which transports her somewhere else. "She forgot the shop, the other customers, her own errand. She forgot the winter air outside, the people going by on the wet pavements. She forgot that she was in London, she forgot the whole of her London life. She seemed to be standing alone in a darkening orchard . . ."

To read this scene in its entirety is in itself hypnotically relaxing. Laura buys a huge bunch of chrysanthemums and in return the grocer gives her a spray of beech leaves. She is practically addicted to their scent. "Where do they come from?" she asks, and that is how she finds her future. She knows instinctively she must go there.

And so she does, amid protestations from her brother and his wife. She rents some rooms in a cottage in Great

Mop and sets about exploring the area, almost frantically. But soon she slows down and life becomes what it was meant to be. She wants hardly anything she knew before. Even her nephew gets on her nerves when he tries to visit; he interrupts her relaxation. Ah, we have found some conflict after all.

Like the women in the paintings I look at, I do most of my reading in bed or on the couch, taking a break from work in the afternoon, or at night before I fall asleep. In winter, I very occasionally put off work for a couple of hours to read in the morning. Reading, then, is almost always relaxing, even if what I'm reading isn't. Even so, there are books I'd never read at night. They are for the morning or afternoon. When the sun goes down, I usually read fiction. Nonfiction for the daylight hours. For poetry, it just depends.

There's a chapter in Claire-Louise Bennett's *Pond* in which the narrator takes a bath; I find myself turning to it often. It's a book I've opened up many times well after my first reading. In fact, it's remained on my desk for months now. I don't think it was written to be relaxing, yet it is. The domestic life described in that book is so mesmerizing, with its bowls of fruit (pears and red currants) and vegetables (aubergine, squash, asparagus, small vine tomatoes) resting on a cold windowsill, and unfinished tapestries sitting darkly on a mantelpiece. But the bath scene in a storm relaxes me most of all.

> A leaf came in through the window and dropped directly onto the water between my knees as I sat in the bath looking out. It was a thoroughly square window and I had it open completely, with the pane pushed right back against the wall. It was there, level with the rim of the bath—I didn't have to stretch or lean.

The detail of the window level with the rim of the bathtub is perfect. Is it not relaxing in its own right? And the fact that it is completely open to the storm? To be in a warm bath and exposed to a storm at the same time. After one gets out of the bath the feeling stays for a while. The same thing happens with reading, of course. When one closes a book it doesn't mean the feeling of the book closes too.

Maybe it's this way our favorite books have of staying with us, but I find myself returning always to Clarice Lispector and Duras, and now Ferrante and Townsend Warner in my thinking, but also when I write, and I've realized that it might make sense to focus on them through writing for an extended period of time. It's said that it only takes a few seconds for the body to tense up, but that to relax completely takes much longer, more like twenty minutes. Maybe spending a long time thinking and writing about a subject allows for a great opportunity of relaxation. Regardless, I also like reading these books because of the state of mind in which they put me.

What else relaxes me? Those paintings of the night, of course; sitting on the deck with Amar at dusk; swimming; Gerald Murnane's *The Plains* ("In moods like this I suspect that every man may be traveling toward the heart of some remote private plain . . ."); standing in front of Walter De Maria's *The Earth Room* in Manhattan; Anna Moschovakis's *They and We Will Get Into Trouble for This*, which almost makes me feel as though I were floating in a sensory deprivation tank ("Samira it's dark outside and winter the branches are thick / with snow I think where there are deserts and olives there / can't be snow but California my mother / land gives me / the lie.").

Of course none of this means we should relax above all else. Now that I have said so much about it, I'm thinking more about who gets to relax, and when, for it is a luxury. If you are someone who relaxes much of the time, maybe you should give some of it away. In Lispector's *The Hour of the Star* there is hardly any rest for Macabéa. If you are as unloved as she is, and as poor, walking in the city might become marked by something else. Still, she is nourished by her daydreams, which must mean she is relaxed by them too, and by the advertisements she cuts out of newspapers and looks at by candlelight. And she's given something else: "Sometimes, grace descended upon her as she sat at her desk in the office. Then she would go to the washroom in order to be alone. Standing and smiling until it passed."

*

I DON'T BELIEVE IN PERFECTION, and when it comes to fiction, it's a value I don't understand. Why should it matter? Is a short story, or a novel, or a work of art, or a film, meant to be perfect? Is it even possible? Do we write in order to create perfect things? I don't. I never think of it when I'm writing. Yet I too have described a work as perfect. Not long ago I declared *Thus Bad Begins* by Javier Marías to be perfection. What did I mean when I said that, and why the compulsion? I suppose I meant I was strongly affected by the novel, which I was. That it exists on a special plane for me, above other books. That it is complete in itself.

When I finished reading *The Days of Abandonment* by Ferrante, I felt a slight disappointment in a novel I had been deeply affected by, that I also think exists on a special plane, and that I had barely been able to put down until the end, that goes convincingly into a place the book itself names "an absence of sense." When the narrator's husband leaves her, she unravels so completely, so grotesquely and violently, I wondered if she would ever come together again. She does come back to herself, and this is also convincing. I was glad for it. It is an absence of sense she suffers, after all, not a complete break in who she is. She says to herself: "The essential thing was that the string, the weave that now supported me, should hold." In our own lives, we never know when the weave that supports us, and our sense of wellbeing, will snap, and what the new support will be. We only know that things change.

Olga's husband thinks that he too has suffered an absence of sense. In fact, this phrase in the novel belongs to him; he is the first one to use it, when, years before, he had also almost left her. At the end of the novel, Olga tells him she doesn't love him anymore because he deceived her by saying he'd fallen into a void. "Now I know what an absence of sense is and what happens if you manage to get back to the surface from it. You, you don't know. At most you glanced down, you got frightened, and you plugged up the hole with Carla's body."

When I read this passage, it felt profound, getting to the difference as it does between escape from the void and the void itself. But the end of the book has a point, it seems: not only do we suffer, we can experience suffering without being totally obliterated by it, and soon afterward we can fall in love with a man we once found repulsive. I was disappointed by this not only because I had loved the book up to this point, but because I don't see Ferrante as a writer concerned with happy endings. That element of sense, coming to love another person, felt forced. In the end, though, I still consider this novel one of my favorites, even if I think it is flawed, even if it in a sense abandons itself, abandons what John Gardner calls in *The Art of Fiction* the fictional dream, that "rich and vivid play in the mind" that comes to the reader through detail. Again and again in novel after novel, plot gets in the way of detail. It destroys the dream.

Still, I'm interested in flaws in works of fiction, in why it is possible to love a book one finds flawed, maybe even more than a book that might be considered "perfect." The truth is that I like *The Days of Abandonment* even more than *Thus Bad Begins*, which, as much as I do like it, is a little distant, cold, sure of itself. *The Days of Abandonment* feels hot, wet, vulgar, and alive, a novel that writhes. But maybe for Ferrante, the writhing wasn't all. Toward the end of the novel, she writes, "The whole future—I thought—will be that way, life lives together with the damp odor of the land of the dead, attention with inattention, passionate leaps of the heart along with abrupt losses of meaning." This is the exact kind of novel I would like to read, the kind of novel I would also like to write.

And there is room, of course. A novel can and should hold different registers of feeling and experience at once, and from that something new can emerge. In Leos Carax's film *Mauvais Sang*, there's a scene of Alex running ecstatically while "Modern Love" by David Bowie blares from the radio. As a young writer, this scene was formative for me, and for that reason I'll never forget it. It showed me something about film, and because I am a writer, it showed me something about writing, that it is possible to almost "leave" the film, leave the book. Along with the writer or the filmmaker, the viewer or the reader enters another kind of space. But it is still the film. It is still the book. The film contains the scene without losing its dream of itself, which I think is incredible. It *is* the dream. Like Jessi Jezewska Stevens's novel *The Exhibition of Persephone Q*, which, for a while, enters a new narrative space three quarters of the way through, almost as if it is becoming a different book. You get the sense that even Percy, the narrator, feels different when she comes through the other side of this space to return to the original. "How far away my fiancé seemed! He was all the way on the other side of the room. It might have been a mile." Like David Lynch's *Mulholland Drive* and the new *Twin Peaks*, works that not only have the ability to leave themselves, but to never come back, to make sense of themselves in a larger, crazier way. A larger, crazier dream. These are the works that exhilarate me. What makes Lynch a genius is that it is impossible to tell the flaw from perfection.

*

COMING BACK RECENTLY TO *ZAZEN* MEDITATION after a number of years away, I remembered how much I love so many of the verses that are chanted in Soto Zen Buddhism. I like them aesthetically, as pieces of writing, and I feel they open something in me that nothing else does, illuminating not just my time in meditation, but my sense of reality. Like "Song of the Precious Mirror Samadhi" (Dongshan Liangjie): "Turning away and touching are both wrong, for it is like a massive fire." And in chanting these verses again, I realize that they've influenced my writing. Not that my fiction is like them, necessarily, but something of them has come through, whether an odd turn of phrase, a kind of austerity, or a pointed image. Until now, I don't think I understood that I connect to the verses not just in how I might think about my life or try to live within it, but creatively too.

I came to writing at the same time that I was coming to *zazen*. I began writing before I began sitting, but I really found my voice as a writer as I was finding my way into Soto Zen Buddhism. At times I've been unable to talk about my process of writing without seeing parallels to my practice of sitting.

For me, the blank page is not unlike the blank wall one faces when sitting in the Soto Zen tradition. There is a clearing of the mind. What's different, of course, is that I'm going to listen to the voice that comes through to me when I'm writing, not gently try to let it go. Still, there's always a process for me in which I make space in a piece of writing, continuously clearing it out, even as a story is arising.

In one of my first *dokusan* (individual interview) meetings with my teacher Taigen Dan Leighton at Ancient Dragon Zen Gate in Chicago, I had a question for him, as we often do in *dokusan*. I have no idea now what the question was. What matters is Taigen's response, which I do remember. He told me I should simply sit with the question. At first, I didn't know what that meant. Was he proposing that I think about the question while sitting *zazen*? No, it meant I should let the question sit with me, without thinking of it. Now it makes sense, and in a way it describes my process of writing. If I have a question about a story or the novel I'm working on, or some issue I'm working through, I usually don't try to solve it through thinking, or even craft. I simply sit with it while I write.

*

I AM READING AN EARLY NOVEL BY RACHEL CUSK, *The Country Life*, about a young woman who escapes her unhappy life in London to work as an au pair. At her new job, Stella makes almost every wrong decision possible and as she does so she has an understanding of these decisions as ones she wouldn't normally make. She is reasonable, almost mousy, or that is what she seems to believe about herself, and what the reader is meant to believe as well. But this is not what the reader is shown of Stella's new life in the country.

It makes me consider what I believe about myself too, and how it might be different from what I actually am, about that distance between what I think and feel and what I sometimes do. The moments in which I act out my anger, for instance. Something happens and I see that I have a choice to get angry or not get angry. If I choose the anger, I am sometimes performing it—in some ways close to it, in other ways removed. I watch myself go through with it. Is it interesting to watch oneself perform? My current answer is that it is not.

The family Stella works for is also "wrong," on many different levels, so perhaps her wrong decisions bring her closer to them. They exist together strangely, Stella and that family; it might be the only way. Maybe wrong is sometimes better. One hot afternoon, badly sunburned and disoriented, Stella cuts a pair of pants into shorts. She cuts them too short and then puts them on in front of a mirror. She looks at herself, for a long time, her body appearing to her as mysterious and unexpectedly erotic. It seems to possess a personality she never knew existed, one that astounds and fascinates her and that she wants to explore. Her desire takes the form of a headache like a "great horn" extending from the front of her head. "With so little about me that I knew, I was virtually unpoliced; and it was in this strange savagery that I began to touch myself in front of the mirror, while the dim protests of my more civilized self went unheeded." I love this scene and what it gets to, the body, and the self, as a territory, that we have a right to upend, with no one to stop us.

Is the self what we've lived through, what we've felt and thought, what we've done? Is it what we've gone toward, or what we haven't gone toward but have instead intensely imagined? If we are writers or artists, is it what we have written or made? Or none of those things? For a while I thought this: that the self is everything that flows through us—thoughts, impressions, emotions, states of being—that we are mediums for life, for experience, while we are here. But none of it stays, none of it is the self in any kind of permanent or total way. If I am anxious I am not anxiety, yet anxiety marks me, marks who I am, how I live. But so does happiness. Now I'm not sure. Maybe the self is the absence of something like anxiety or happiness. Maybe we carry things that don't actually belong to us. Somehow we can't put them down. But, whether we are carrying them or not, they exist outside us.

It's impossible to know what the self is. There is so much that could be responsible for it, and so much that gets in the way. Which parts are able to come forward, to exist actively, and which stay latent? If I lived differently, would different aspects of my self come to the foreground? Or is the self—the true self—more dominant than behavior, than habits?

What has the self been in fiction? It is too big a question. It might make sense to look at a very short piece of writing to answer it. As the narrator in Borges's one page story "Borges and I" remarks: "My taste runs to hourglasses, maps, eighteenth-century typefaces, etymologies, the taste of coffee, and the prose of Robert Louis Stevenson; Borges shares those preferences, but in a vain sort of way that turns them into the accoutrements of an actor." It is a melancholy piece of writing, regretful. These two selves that divide Borges seem to cause sadness in at least one of them. If the other self were speaking, what would he say? Can a more authentic self see another that is fake? Did the soul of Borges regret the Borges that was a famous writer? Now writers brand themselves online, as corporations do. I am afraid that this damages the self, or at the very least, that if we engage in it we are trading in some part of the self for something false, and that the more we trade in, the more of the self we lose.

There is also the issue of interference, distraction. What part of the self browses the Internet? What is that self trying to get to? I admit that I look online a lot when I am writing. I check my email, look at Twitter or Instagram, and then I look at clothes. I don't know if my writing has suffered because of this, is simply different than it would have been without these interruptions, or if my writing is able to come through no matter what. It's strange how in touch you can be now with other writers as you work, and readers, and editors, and agents, and booksellers, if you choose that, at any point in the day. What does it mean to be so frequently in a literary conversation, and if not in conversation oneself, then watching one unfold, or re-tweeting it, broadcasting it, to those who "follow" you, and what does it mean to be so in conversation *while writing* when the distracted writer finds themself online?

I wonder if the Internet is shifting the borders of the self, or if the self is just filtered through it. Joanna Walsh's *Break.up* meditates on (the end of) a relationship that takes place mostly online, through emails and texts. It is about a relationship, but also *this* kind of a relationship, that exists mostly through writing. When the couple is not together (they live in different countries and are not together very often at all), the narrator prefers email or texting to talking on the phone. "Type, at least, has memory. Give me the cold keys of my aluminum laptop and I'll play them like a Belleville piano. What's more, writing gives me time for some elegance of response (*elegance is refusal*), for some *esprit d'éscalier*, in the timelapse." It seems to me that in this kind of relationship one is able to retain one's aloneness, and all that that entails, both positive and negative. An intense connection that can come at any time, day or night, a back and forth, or just once: a quick sentence, a long letter. But one receives it while alone. And when the connection wanes or is pulled back from, the typing wanes too. If our relationships can be different in this way now, I think we must be different too.

There are two scenes from *Mrs Dalloway* that I sometimes see in my mind. Clarissa gazing out of her bedroom window before her party begins, and then in the middle of it, while it is taking place. It's something I myself have always done and enjoyed, taking a break at parties. There's something comforting about being by oneself in the midst of being with people, and then it is pleasurable to go back out if the party itself is pleasurable. To be alone, and then with people, side by side. This small, interior moment inside of a larger, exterior one: "Big Ben struck the half-hour. How extraordinary it was, strange, yes, touching, to see the old lady (they had been neighbors ever so many years) move away from the window, as if she were attached to that sound, that string. Gigantic as it was, it had something to do with her."

To be that old woman, watched tenderly by chance, in that simple, private moment. What is revealed in it? To be Clarissa Dalloway seeing her neighbor pulled away from the window by the sound of the clock. Clarissa is alone too. It is the reader who sees her. The reader, coming from this other time, the present. To truly see another. To be seen. I think that is when we feel most loved, close to someone. When Clarissa looks at the old woman, in some way she is seeing her own self. Not in the other woman. In herself seeing another. In her time alone, just like the woman is alone in that moment.

From Sheila Heti's *Motherhood*: "Alone, one feels the whole universe, and none of one's personality." A personality, sometimes it is a burden. How nice it can feel to set it down. For it to momentarily disappear. Maybe this is partly what is meant by letting go of the self. It is one way we can do it.

The self changes, always; we can't keep it in place. So, instead of self—selves. In the novel *Savage Tongues* by Azareen Van der Vliet Oloomi, the self is explored relentlessly, lovingly, when the narrator, Arezu, returns to a site of trauma and eroticism, her father's terrible and dreary apartment in Marbella, Spain, which he has now handed down to her, as empty of him as it was twenty years before when she spent the summer there alone, and with Omar, her father's wife's nephew. The apartment is haunted, not just by Omar and the acts that transpired there, but most significantly, perhaps, by the girl Arezu was then, abandoned in a way that was like a death. At the end of her weekend in that place so strongly imprinted by the past, Arezu looks out the window at the palm trees and aloe plants and buildings and ruins and feels herself become two different people, seeing for the first time through the eyes of the girl she'd been and the woman she now is. "My vision felt doubly powerful. Her heart was beating alongside mine. It was trembling, fearful, unsure of itself, but also eager to leave. I could feel her resolve rising to match mine." In *Savage Tongues,* the self we once were joins with who we are, they needn't be separate, even if it seems at times there is a gulf between them. We come to understand that healing is possible.

*

WHILE THINKING AND WRITING ABOUT NOVELS and short stories, I've mostly been paying attention to things we could say are "accessories" to them, not to what we would say is crucial. I haven't been paying attention to plot, character, dialogue, or conflict, those formal elements of fiction. If I get to these elements at all, it is through one of these accessories, like animals, relaxation, friendship, or the self. Animals appear in novels just as characters do, even if not all of the time. Plants appear in fiction too. I've begun to think that when they appear, they can guide us in understanding what we are reading, and where we are when we read.

In fiction, I like description very much, but not just any kind of description, as sometimes it can be too utilitarian to be interesting, to heighten something, to do more than simply show the reader what they should see in their mind as they read. The best kinds of description evoke feeling, and not just emotional feeling, but a sense of something *else*, a different kind of knowing. Descriptions of plants in fiction are especially nice because they have the potential to be a representation of a number of things, like nature itself, or wildness, but also lushness and health. And in the same way that plants enrich the environments where we spend our time, and clean the air, they can enrich settings in fiction, altering them. Living with plants changes the house I'm in, changes me, and part of why I like Southern California so much is because of the plants that grow here. When I walk in the mountains, or go to the desert, it feels like something changes in my brain, and I become a more serene, looser version of myself. I wonder if reading about plants can do that too.

The Book of Feral Flora by Amanda Ackerman is, as you might guess, about wild plants, and though I wouldn't categorize the book exclusively as fiction, it is in relationship to fiction, it is "near fiction" no doubt, and as a fiction writer I am interested in this nearness. It is also near poetry. One of the most exciting aspects of the book, though, as the "Process Notes" state, is that some of the pieces were written by plants, plants like Iris and Morning Glory. You will have to read *The Book of Feral Flora* to find out more about how this happened, but I will say at least that it involved somatic devices and recordings and sensors. The flowers in the book call out to other flowers, repeating their names, making contact, one to the other. Ackerman calls out to them too. This is one kind of feralness.

But it is not just plants like Iris and Morning Glory that appear in *The Book of Feral Flora*, it is weeds, to which the book is dedicated. "There are weeds on the land, weeds in the air, and weeds in the sea." They are everywhere, of course; we try to make them not be. Weeds are unwanted, and, Ackerman writes, they compete with the kinds of plants people wish to have in their gardens. In "Weed Course," the narrator plants her own garden, and inevitably weeds sprout up and grow tall and fast. "I wanted to call them pretty but they were weeds." This is another kind of feralness.

For a while, I went to the Huntington Gardens almost every week. It is the only botanical garden I've visited so regularly. Each time I go, I walk through different parts of it, overlapping them. I've been through every section, but it took me a long time to find the herb garden; it was invisible to me and somehow I missed it. I found it while walking in the more popular rose garden with Amanda Ackerman. Actually, it was she who found it. The cactus forest I have walked through many times, also very popular. Usually I go to the Huntington with Amar, who is researching and writing a book about early botanical expeditions. I also go there alone, sometimes to write, and now the plants are starting to stay in my consciousness. I can feel how I am connecting to them, and they to me. I'm excited because this has never happened before.

Once I had a similar relationship to the Art Institute of Chicago, twice weekly visits, each time walking through different galleries, different rooms, but always overlapping

them. The eternal return. This is how I describe my relationship to writing, and to meditation. I do not always do them,
or at least not everyday, but I always return, and in that way
they are constants. I absorbed something in my many visits to those galleries, in the same way I am now absorbing
something in my return to the gardens.

At home, Amar is growing orchids, hoyas, jasmine, different kinds of succulents and cacti, manzanita, yarrow,
other native plants, plants that are native to Australia and
New Zealand, where the climate is similar to this one. I am
lucky to have so many plants around me. On my own, I don't
raise them very well. The orchids are in a garden window in
our kitchen and planted outside, the hoyas in the bedroom,
there is a fern hanging in my small study. In winter, Amar
brings in a few of the hoyas from outside and hangs them
from the beams in our living room. Our courtyard is full
of plants, in the ground, and hanging. There are huge birds
of paradise plants that look like NDiaye's banana tree, and
ginger. It's tropical, which I like. More plants are growing in
the front and side yards, the yarrow and manzanita, which
are under our olive tree, the plants from New Zealand, huge
cacti. Our hillside is feral, taken over by jade and sage, and

by weeds. I am surrounded by plants here. I can feel this
when I sit down at my desk to write.

Reading Ann Radcliffe's *The Mysteries of Udolpho*, I was as
enthralled with her lengthy descriptions of the landscape
as I was with the mystery and horror of the story. I was attached to the plot, I'll admit (though I don't like the way it
wraps itself up in the end); it's not that I'm never drawn to
story. But the plants in this novel, and the landscapes, are so
detailed it is stunning. Radcliffe draws a full picture of them,
lingers so long in them, you feel that she also found them
important to the story she was telling. Or, it was just the style
of the times. I wish it still was.

The novel begins with a description of the countryside,
and by the second sentence we have already begun to read
of what grows there, including many olive trees. Emily, the
protagonist, has a room all to herself bordering the east side
of the greenhouse, in which she keeps her books and drawings and instruments, and her own favorite plants. "The
windows of this room were particularly pleasant; they descended to the floor, and opening upon the little lawn that
surrounded the house, the eye was led between groves of

almond, palm-trees, flowering-ash, and myrtle, to the distant landscape, where the Garonne wandered."

As Emily travels through the Pyrenees and the Apennines on her way to her gothic castle, we see even more of the scenery and, by extension, the plants. Without that immersion, the reader would never be able to feel to such an extent where they are, with that kind of profuseness. The castle too is explored in all its frightening detail, surrounded by that rich natural world we've already come to know so well. We have been situated in it. We feel its presence even when we're inside.

Cusk does some version of this with rain in her novel *Arlington Park*. For five pages, before any of the main characters are introduced, we read (watch) a heavy spring shower in a suburb of London. The reader is steeped in the storm, in Arlington Park, before moving to the story. It changes the reader's relationship to the setting, and even to the characters. I don't think we are meant to relate to them and their shallowness, and this way of beginning sets that up. The rain is deeper than they are, and the reader is outside in it; we too feel caught in the storm. We see what surrounds the characters before we see them, we see them get wet. And though there will not be quite this focus on rain again, it will rain through the whole novel. Recently, someone reminded me that Charlotte Brontë's *Villette* ends with a storm, so I went back to read that ending again. "The skies hang full and dark—a rack sails from the west; the clouds cast themselves into strange forms—arches and broad radiations . . ." Soon, it will storm for a week without stopping.

So too does the bonsai appear toward the end of Alejandro Zambra's novel of the same name. There is something nice about having this access to the natural world, to remembering that it can have value in a work of fiction, just as it does in our lives. What if a work of fiction simply ended with pages and pages of descriptions of plants? If it doesn't already exist, I think I must sit down and write it.

*

FOR A LONG TIME I'VE BEEN THINKING about what it means to fall apart, for a piece of writing to fall apart. As a person, does it mean that the pieces of myself I try to keep together just can't do it in that moment, that they need for their own relief to be separate, pure in themselves in some way? At least for a while, before I try to bring them together again. And writing in a way that is unrefined, vulnerable, not interested in craft, is it also a kind of falling apart, a refusal to keep things together? Sometimes I'm real and sometimes I'm not real. Sometimes I'm alienated from my true nature and sometimes I am my true nature. I don't like the alienation, but to feel it, and then to find it lifted, I wonder if that is valuable too. To know the difference, to not stay stuck.

Am I "pure" when I write, am I real, am I my true nature? It's one of the times when I am *not* alienated from myself; maybe that's why I like writing so much. If you are not alienated from yourself, you are more likely to go further into the thing on which you are working. At least I think that's right. In an interview with Elissa Schappell in *Vanity Fair*, when Ferrante is asked if she knows ahead of time what shape one of her books will take, she says the only thing she knows from the outset is that it must be driven by a strong sense of truth. "If, even for a few passages, the tone becomes false—that is, too studied, too limpid, too regimented, too well-phrased—I am obliged to stop and to figure out where I started to go wrong. If I can't, I throw everything away." In the last year, this kind of truth has become more important to me, as a writer, than anything else. Going further into my writing means being vigilant about shedding what is false, even the smallest bit of it. Sometimes sentences I have written in the past make me cringe, even if I once liked them. They might sound okay, but they're hollow, with nothing behind them. I have already cut many false sentences from this book, but I'm afraid there will be more I'm not yet capable of seeing. I already write such short, sparse texts. How much more can I get rid of?

I want to be able to write about loneliness, humiliation, and shame, things I never would have written about before, that would have embarrassed me. For a long time I didn't want to write "emotionally." I dislike many representations of love and dramatic feeling in writing, and I didn't want to replicate them. And there has been something valuable for me in exploring the emotionless. Part of what I like about Cusk's writing is that she writes extensively of emotions, but without being emotional. I myself have always been an emotional person, but I've wanted to think that my writing might be driven by something different, and often it has, but I'd be lying if I said emotion wasn't important to me now. I see value in it too. In my writing, why not be fully who I am? I can't stay only in one place, and I can't stay on the surface of my writing life. I used to worry I was not an intellectual in the same ways many of my friends were, not wanting to admit that I sometimes couldn't completely understand them when they were so fluidly in conversation with each other. I listened quietly in those moments, aware of the means by which I feel my way toward things, even thought. My writing is like that too.

I want to write more of closeness and intimacy, especially given how much in the past I have written of awkwardness and distance. I don't want to stay on the surface of language, the surface of sentences. I want intimacy and sentences both, which is why I love the work of writers like Cusk, Ferrante, and Suzanne Scanlon. All three have changed what I thought I wanted in writing. At the start of *Her 37th Year, An Index*, Scanlon quotes E.M. Cioran, something along the lines of only writing books if they contain the things you'd never actually say in your life (though my goal is for both: to write them and say them). Scanlon, whose narrator tells her therapist she desires sleep, God, travel, transcendence, who says she has always written "as if trying to love." I have not gone far enough, in my writing or my life, and in that way I haven't told the truth.

I want to write like Anne Carson in "The Glass Essay," when she describes being left by Law, when she takes off her clothes and turns away from him because she knows he likes her back: "Everything I know about love and its necessities / I learned in that one moment / when I found myself / thrusting my little burning red backside like a baboon / at a man who no longer cherished me." I want to write with that kind of force and pain and genuineness and beauty, for it is a beautiful moment, Carson's awareness of it, at least, and the way she writes afterwards about the soul and watches it. I want to write with that kind of expansiveness, into one's life and the landscape one is in. It is like a needle piercing the sky. Writing of spending time with one's mother, the conversations they have in a spring that is really a late brutal winter, not understood by her mother at all. Loneliness on the moors, becoming Emily Brontë, ice and interiors, the house and the mind, Emily's siblings and characters coming to life in this other way, in Carson's writing. I admire it, and I feel so much when I read it, but how can I feel cradled in something so difficult? It's the writing itself that does that, the details, the setting, the cutting through, taking off one's clothes.

I don't want to turn away from difficulty of any kind in my writing, not just that of shame and vulnerability. There are larger, deeper difficulties ahead. The acute effects of climate change are with us now, are already changing our experiences. There may be other pandemics. When it comes to how and what I write, I can't ignore that, which would be its own kind of falseness; to just continue on, writing about the things I once did as though nothing had changed, even if at one time they seemed like enough, even if they once mattered to me.

When I read Marlen Haushofer's *The Wall*, at first I was afraid of it; I knew it would be emotionally hard. Now *there* is loneliness, a woman living only for survival, terrifyingly isolated, everyone she knows disappeared and assumed dead. Of course it's not true that she's totally alone. She has animals with her—a dog, cats, a cow—animals she loves deeply. Though most of them die too, which is heartbreaking, and with their deaths she does become more and more alone. I don't even like novels of the apocalypse, and have never wanted to write one, but I couldn't put this book down. It was a compulsive, dread-filled kind of reading. It depressed me, but I cared about it. How exactly to write about this level of difficulty, I am still figuring out. I begin to think that I must write a novel of suffering because so many are suffering, and because many more of us certainly will, but I don't know yet if that is it.

I used to feel such joy all the time; I didn't know it would change. I used to think that once you felt intense happiness, it would only grow stronger, that once discovered it would keep opening up and out, that experience was like this too, that life became more and more open to you. Naively, I didn't anticipate a closing down. Scanlon writes about something like this in *Her 37ᵗʰ Year*, referencing the movie version of Michael Cunningham's *The Hours*, when Meryl Streep's character is talking about her life to her daughter: "I remember thinking, this was the beginning of happiness. But no, that was it. That wasn't the beginning." And Cusk too, in *Outline,* through the life of the man her narrator meets on the plane on her way to Greece, who in the early parts of the novel talks extensively of the breakdown of his first marriage and of an early belief in plenitude:

> He and his wife had built things that had flourished, had together expanded the sum of what they were and what they had; life had responded willingly to them, had treated them abundantly, and this—he now saw—was what had given him the confidence to break it all, break it with what now seemed to him to be an extraordinary casualness, because he thought there would be more.

I feel such relief reading passages like this. I've always been moved to write of the happiness I've experienced, and have likewise found happiness a pleasure to read. I'm surprised to be just as drawn to writing that details the breakdown of happiness too. If not pleasurable exactly, there is a strong sense of recognition and meaning in it, something I want to explore. And now I know. You take hold of your happiness and enjoy it when it is with you. You experience it with gratitude, knowing nothing lasts. Now when I am happy, which gratefully I still am, when I am having a good time, I think about how lucky I am. I feel this even, and especially, during the pandemic. When I look around at the house I share with my husband, or we sit on our deck together in the evenings, looking out at the hills, having a drink, like my grandfather Lucien used to do with his wife Betty, on his porch overlooking the Smoky Mountains, a wave of extreme thankfulness washes over me. I think, if I die soon I had this life.

If I can't write climate fiction, I think, I can at least write of that breaking down. Of falling apart. And I think that that is what I'll do. And I'll write about the things that make me feel ashamed at this point in my life, like getting older, not being who I once was, and I think that this will be healing.

But now that I am working on a new novel, I am not writing about shame at all. For the first time, it is love I seem to want to write about. I am still interested in pleasure. I am still interested in landscape. But how can I, how will I, write about these things now? I don't think I have to figure it out beforehand; my subconscious mind is leading me. Already, under the pleasure, under the tropical landscape of the novel, I can see something ominous starting to arise. I have never been able to force myself to write about anything, or to avoid anything for that matter, and I don't think I ever will, so I'll just see what keeps arising, how I approach the difficulties of being alive in this particular moment in time. Once again, it's freedom I want when it comes to writing, and in life, even within responsibility. Being unrestrained. Yet I know it will be different; it always is. Like a horse standing in darkness. The pasture gate has been left open.

Works Cited

Ackerman, Amanda. *The Book of Feral Flora*. Los Angeles: Les Figues Press, 2015.

Arendt, Hannah. *The Life of the Mind*. 1971. San Diego: Harcourt, 1978.

Bennett, Claire-Louise. *Pond*. New York: Riverhead, 2015.

Bolaño, Roberto. *The Third Reich*. 2010. Translated by Natasha Wimmer. New York: Farrar, Straus and Giroux, 2011.

Borges, Jorge Luis. "Borges and I," *Collected Fictions*. Translated by Andrew Hurley. New York: Penguin, 1998.

Brontë, Charlotte. *Jane Eyre*. 1847. London: Penguin Classics, 2009.

_____. *Villette*. 1853. New York: Signet Classics, 2014.

Bryant, Tisa. *Unexplained Presence*. Providence: Leon Works, 2007.

Byatt, A.S. *Portraits in Fiction*. New York: Vintage, 2001.

Calvino, Italo. *Six Memos for the Next Millennium*. 1988. Translated by Patrick Creagh. New York: Vintage, 1993.

Carson, Anne. "The Glass Essay," *Glass, Irony & God*. New York: New Directions, 1995.

Cusk, Rachel. *The Country Life*. London: Picador, 1997.

_____. *Outline*. New York: Farrar, Straus and Giroux, 2015.

Donato, Claire. *Burial*. Grafton: Tarpaulin Sky Press, 2013.

Duras, Marguerite. *Blue Eyes, Black Hair*. Translated by Barbara Bray. New York: Pantheon Books, 1987.

_____. *The Ravishing of Lol Stein*. 1964. Translated by Richard Seaver. New York: Pantheon Press, 1966.

Ernaux, Annie. *The Possession*. 2002. Translated by Anna Moschovakis. New York: Seven Stories Press, 2008.

Ferrante, Elena. *The Days of Abandonment*. 2002. Translated by
Ann Goldstein. New York: Europa Editions, 2005.

_____. *The Lost Daughter*. 2006. Translated by Ann Goldstein. New
York: Europa Editions, 2008.

Gardner, John. *The Art of Fiction*. 1983. New York: Vintage, 1991.

Genet, Jean. *The Maids and Deathwatch*. 1954. Translated by Ber-
nard Frechtman. New York: Grove Press, 1982.

Gladman, Renee. *Ana Patova Crosses a Bridge*. St. Louis: Dorothy,
a publishing project, 2013.

_____. *Calamities*. Seattle: Wave Books, 2016.

Gopnik, Adam. *Winter*. Toronto: House of Anansi Press, 2011.

Heti, Sheila. *Motherhood*. New York: Henry Holt, 2018.

Humphreys, Helen. *The Frozen Thames*. 2007. New York: Dela-
corte Press, 2009.

Ishiguro, Kazuo. *A Pale View of Hills*. 1982. New York: Vintage,
1990.

Jansson, Tove. *The True Deceiver*. 1982. Translated by Thomas Teal.
New York: NYRB, 2009.

Jaeggy, Fleur. "Portrait of an Unknown Woman," *I Am the Brother
of XX*. 2015. Translated by Gini Alhadeff. New York: New Directions, 2017.

Liangjie, Dongshan. "Song of the Precious Mirror Samadhi," *Culti-
vating the Empty Field: The Silent Illumination of Zen Master
Hongzhi*. Translated by Taigen Dan Leighton with Yi Wu. Bos-
ton: Tuttle Publishing, 2000.

Lispector, Clarice. *The Hour of the Star*. 1977. Translated by Giovanni
Pontiero. New York: New Directions, 1986.

MacLane, Mary. *I Await the Devil's Coming*. 1902. New York: Mel-
ville House, 2013.

Morrison, Toni. *Beloved*. 1987. New York: Vintage, 2004.

Moschovakis, Anna. *They and We Will Get into Trouble for This*. Minneapolis: Coffee House Press, 2016.

Murnane, Gerald. 1982. *The Plains*. Melbourne: Text Classics, 2017.

NDiaye, Marie. *Self-Portrait in Green*. 2005. Translated by Jordan Stump. San Francisco: Two Lines Press, 2014.

Nunez, Sigrid. *The Friend*. New York: Riverhead, 2018.

Pamuk, Orhan. *The Naïve and the Sentimental Novelist*. 2010. Translated by Nazim Dikbaş. London: Faber and Faber, 2011.

Pick, Anat. *Creaturely Poetics*. New York: Columbia University Press, 2011.

Radcliffe, Ann. *The Mysteries of Udolpho*. 1794. New York: Penguin Classics, 2001.

Samatar, Sofia. "Olimpia's Ghost," *Tender*. Easthampton: Small Beer Press, 2017.

Scanlon, Suzanne. *Her 37th Year, An Index*. Blacksburg: Noemi Press, 2015.

Stevens, Jessi Jezewska. *The Exhibition of Persephone Q*. New York: Farrar, Straus and Giroux, 2020.

Tanizaki, Junichiro. *In Praise of Shadows*. 1933. Translated by Thomas J. Harper and Edward G. Seidensticker. New York: Vintage, 2001.

Townsend Warner, Sylvia. *Lolly Willowes; or The Loving Huntsman*. 1926. New York: NYRB, 1999.

Van der Vliet Oloomi, Azareen. *Savage Tongues*. New York: Mariner Books, 2021.

Walsh, Joanna. *Break.up*. South Pasadena: Semiotext(e), 2018.

―――. "Vagues," *Vertigo*. St. Louis: Dorothy, a publishing project, 2015.

Woolf, Virginia. *Mrs Dalloway*. New York: Harcourt, 1925.

_____. *The Waves*. New York: Harcourt, 1931.

_____. *A Writer's Diary*. New York: Harcourt, 1953.

Zambreno, Kate. *Drifts*. New York: Riverhead, 2021.

Acknowledgments

Thank you to the editors of the publications where excerpts of this work appeared in earlier form: Hayden Bennett at the *Believer Logger*, Nadja Spiegelman and Sadie Stein at the *Paris Review Daily*, Hermione Thompson at *Five Dials*, Josie Mitchell at *Granta*, Medaya Ocher at the *Los Angeles Review of Books*, Sessily Watt at *Puerto del Sol*, Meagan Day and Helen Stuhr-Rommereim at *Full Stop*, and Lauren Spohrer at *Two Serious Ladies*.

Thank you to Patrick Cottrell, Kate Zambreno, Sofia Samatar, Adam Novy, Kate Durbin, Hayden Bennett, Adrienne Walser, Stacy Dacheaux, Alex Branch, and Laida Lertxundi, who have been over the years my favorite people to talk to about books and writing and art, and to Amarnath Ravva, Colin Dickey, Jason Brown, David Eng, and Ariana Kelly, who, through their writing and their talks at Betalevel in Los Angeles, taught me something important about the essay and nonfiction. As always, thank you to Mel Flashman.

Most of all I want to thank Danielle Dutton and Martin Riker. This book wouldn't exist in quite this way without them, both because of what visionaries and fine editors they are, but also because of the very project of Dorothy. They've helped me go further in my thinking about fiction, about what it can look like and be.

About the Author

Amina Cain is the author of two collections of stories—*Creature* (Dorothy, a publishing project, 2013) and *I Go To Some Hollow* (Les Figues Press, 2009)—and the novel *Indelicacy* (Farrar, Straus and Giroux, 2020), which was a *New York Times* Editors' Choice and a finalist for the Rathbones Folio Prize and the Center for Fiction's First Novel Prize. She lives in Los Angeles with her husband, the writer Amarnath Ravva.